ONE LIFE...
AND THEN SOME

Epiphany 2003

To Nigel:

Valued Fellow Pilgrim

in my Later Life

warm regards,

Gordon

5949-GRAH

ONE LIFE...

AND THEN SOME

1 The Sowing

Rev. Dr. Gordon Graham

5949-GRAH

To order additional copies of this book, contact:
Xlibris Corporation
1-888-795-4274
www.Xlibris.com
Orders@Xlibris.com

CONTENTS

To everything there is a season,
A time for every matter under Heaven:
A time to be born,
A time to die;
A time to plant,
And a time to pluck up what is planted ...

Ecclesiastes 3:1-2

FORWARD

It must be the Irish in me. In setting down my story, I have decided not to let the facts get in the way of a good story. Indeed, now that I wear the collar of an ordained cleric and am called upon to do exegesis of scripture weekly, I offer my theological justification. The Bible, I assure you, contains a collection of stories having little by way of actual facts therein. However, they are told and retold to our great benefit for the universal Truths and moral instruction they contain rather than for the facts. And so it is with my narrative herein. Let go of any quarrel you might have with the facts presented and open yourself to the larger truths which I have striven diligently to share.

Also, in assembling these memories, I am keenly aware that some of the people mentioned or their loved ones will remember things quite differently than I have. So, by and large, I disclaim any special or privileged insight into these people. In several cases, the subject has become more of a concept and thus really a composite of several people who affected me in some way. In other cases, I have encountered substantial people who shaped me in my entire being. These individuals may well have been split into several.

However, some people deserve to be painted just as they appeared to me. I claim no other knowledge of these people than my direct experience with them, but they will be named and called what I think they deserve to be called. For any hurt thus caused, I apologize.

ACKNOWLEDGMENTS

Unconfirmed memories all too often lapse into illusions. As I undertook to recollect these early formative years, I turned first to my cousins and kinfolk. On the maternal side, my cousin Dorothy Freeman Holmes provided considerable material on the Cummings family, in Ireland and in America. This confirmed the wonderful discoveries I had made in the Christ Church Castlebar school records so kindly opened to me by the Rev. Gary Hastings, its present rector, counselor and seminary field work supervisor. On the paternal I found the records now maintained by Joan McCullough, the diligent and heroic archivist of the McCullough/Graham Association (on whose Board first I, then son Chris, and now daughter Rachel serve), supplemented by records and memories generously shared by Cousin Sally McCullough Johnson, allowed me to sort out the huge and still expanding Ulster tribe from whom my father sprang, some still in Ireland and those who, like Sally and I, are descendents of immigrants.

To corroborate those joyous yet stressful days in primary school I owe much to written materials shared with me by Marjorie Burgwinkle Bashaw, David Kirk, Aristea Biskaduros Georgeson, and Loretta Karras Dunbar, whose shared memories included not only Parkhurst School, but also the Free Methodist Church community of the 1940s and that formative phenomenon of the Palmer Camp Meeting.

Lifelong friendships with Tony Mosa (CHS '52) and Henry Brousseau and Leo McNamara (CHS '50) brought vividly to mind the experiences we shared. Caroline Keiger and Mary Jaquith LeSueur offered from the other side of the then rigid gender divide their lasting impressions of that wonderful Class of '51.

Then those who offered me the time and space to begin writing this modest work. First and foremost to my wife and lover of these now 4⅟ years Barbara Sutton Graham, who has always shared with me the importance of giving each other time and space. As of this writing she remains in Ireland having generously provided me a three month "leave of absence" before rejoining me for the CHS '51s Fiftieth. I am grateful also to my Irish Bishop, the Rt. Rev. Harold Miller, for granting me a six-month sabbatical so that I could accept the kind invitation of Barbara MacDougall of St. Ann By-the Sea, on Block Island, to hole up in St. Ann's lovely rectory for six months, with only duties being Sunday Services.

For technical, layout, and illustration support I have turned to my old friend and former client Richard Lowell Harding, whose photography on command, brings vivid life to my chronicle. Terry Ingano of the Clinton Historical Society provided access to the records he lovingly guards. John and Lesley Sisto, proprietors of Block Island's Book Nook Bookstore, gave generously of their time and talents to help me conceptualize and realize artwork of this book.

Tribute need also be made to the works of Erik H. Erickson, Freudian psychoanalyst and prolific author, all of whose works I read immediately preceding putting down these memories. His last work, co-authored with his wife Joan, is aptly entitled "The Life Cycle Completed". I have made my own his conceptualization of life's stages and am comfortably reconciled to make the most of this last cycle – with the Goal he characterizes as "Integrity", by which we may, with courage, fend off the besetting twin temptations of Despair and Disdain. From Erikson's concepts I understand now how in the rich milieu of early life experience I learned to love and trust. Special thanks go to Dr. Richard Ingram who carries on the embattled Freudian tradition in Downshire Hospital in Northern Ireland who graciously cut back his fee schedule so that I could try out these reminiscences first on his couch and attach to them the perspective which uninhibited emotions can made valid.

Finally, there is my newly re-discovered second cousin Patricia Douglas who felicitously re entered my life over the year preceding my writing. Pat, providentially, found herself and her Hollywood actor boss, between assignments on the West Coast and without much arm twisting was persuaded to come East to Block Island for these final two weeks of February 2001 and make order out of the chaos in which she found this effort of reminiscence. The final product is as much her work as mine – indeed the best of it is hers and the remainder has been sent to press over her good judgment.

And to Him/Her who is the Prime Source and Sustainer of my being I give thanks for the good health and blessings of life, which have brought me to this point of looking back with thanksgiving.

INTRODUCTION

Clinton Central Park

in the rearview mirror

Autumn 2000 and I was returning to America for a month. I had been asked by my Harvard classmates to lead a Memorial Service in Cambridge and I was honored to do so. I would be spending this time alone and was joyfully anticipating this unique opportunity to rediscover my past and renew old acquaintances. The month was already packed with plans to return to boyhood haunts and long-forgotten secret places of heart and home.

My first Sunday home was celebrated with the biennial Graham/McCullough Family reunion, a grand gathering of dozens of first and second cousins.

I was extended invitations to preach the following weekend at both Clinton's Congregation Shaari Zadeck Synagogue and Good Shepard Church. Friday afternoon, in anticipation of dinner that evening with old school chums, I found myself visiting the new Clinton High School, now in its second reincarnation from the one I graduated from in 1951. Later that afternoon I spent some time visiting a classmate who was one of my first crushes in the eighth grade and Peter Kamataris, the local barber whose daughter had been my secretary at my first Clinton law office. He was a wealth of information and stories of Clinton in the 1940s.

Later I strolled through Central Park to the rebuilt park fountain bringing back flashes of memories of seeing the original one crushed the frightful night of the 1938 hurricane. Passing the post office I observed its still conspicuous cornerstone, placed at its dedication by James Farley, FDR's Postmaster General in 1937. I recollected how that celebration had been briefly interrupted when my mother and I were asked to move from our prime seats for the festivities – atop the ceremonial cornerstone itself! I walked on to the restored Corcoran School, home for my seventh grade year and now an assisted living center for the elderly. There I happened across Angelo Despotopolous, the nephew and namesake of Angelo, the Forest Street fruit vendor, who appeared weekly in my boyhood East Street neighborhood.

That evening's dinner was filled with faces from my past – Al Cooperman, a longtime friend from Primary school, his wife and cousins of Annalie Haberman, a young lady whom I courted in my teens under the Jewish alias Gordon Schwartz , with the connivance of the Cooperman family. I was jokingly referred to as their cousin from New York.

Saturday, after the synagogue service, I had breakfast with the Coopermans and the Goulds. George Gould reminded me of my visit to his haberdashery when I was eight and my mother had brought me in for my first long-trousered suit.

Sunday morning as I made my way to Good Shepherd Church, I drove down North High Street past the former Free Methodist Church which my father helped to build in our backyard in 1925 and on past Parkhurst School where I was enrolled in 1939 for grades one through five. Adjacent to Parkhurst, still finely groomed and green, now all but abandoned stood Fuller Field, site of many of my youthful football victories, sadly this year for the first time in fifty, no longer home to the mythical Galloping Gaels.

As the weekend progressed, my mind raced through the many people, places and events that formed me. I looked back as if in a rearview mirror. All mirrors, of course, distort. Things distant may look closer. Things that once stood tall are flattened. This was how this account took form.

It will start and most likely one day end in Clinton, Massachusetts. Boston, Cambridge, Ft. Dix, New Jersey, Ft. Holabird, Md. Grosse Reiter Kaserne, Stuttgart, Germany, Washington D.C., Manassas, Virginia and now County Down, Ireland will all play supporting roles. But it was Clinton that bore me, Clinton that shaped me, Clinton that both accepted and limited me and it's the people of Clinton that have remained the constants of my life. To them this book is dedicated.

CHAPTER 1
MY HOMETOWN

Clinton Town Hall

about clinton

Clinton's Century

In Nashua's fertile valley, one hundred years ago
When woods were full of game and living costs were low.
When oil lamps lighted houses, the horse transported man;
Clinton town was founded. Her history began.

Among her hills there settled men of courage, faith and skill
Who toiled with hand and brain, in office, shop and mill.
Soon her looms were humming, weaving cottons, wool, and wires
And secrets of her dye rooms were taught be skillful dryers.

Lofty elms o'er topping church spires from her sod
Were raised by men and women who loved and feared their God.
Midst houses filled with children, busy red-brick schools
Were weighing Clinton's future, and shaping freedom's tools.

The White House used her carpets, her wire fenced Western farms,
And ginghams? Oh, her ginghams were one of women's charms
In Senate's courts and churches spoke her eloquent sons.
And daughters? Were framed as handsome ones.

Unhappily for Clinton the day of mergers came,
Control of her mills went Westward and with it went its fame.
Looms were still; fires burned low; faces were tired and sad.
Men sought work to feed their fires, but work could not be had.

Amid her hills still dwelt men of courage, faith and skill.
They strove with might and blessed by Divine Will.
Again her mills were running, making plastics, books and lights
Faith had conquered darkness. Skill set ruin to rights.

Her century behind her, Clinton looks ahead.
Good of her past remembered; bad, if any, dead.
A second Century's calling, through rainbow arch of years,
Onward, upward, Clinton, march forward without fears.

Anonymous
Town of Clinton Centennial Book 1950

Thus wrote the local secular hymnist in my last year in Clinton
High. Here in Clinton, thanks to the courageous emigration of
Lillian Cumming and George Graham, I came to be planted, to
grow and be nourished in preparation for harvest.

We never questioned the conceit of Clinton's uniqueness and
there were facts to support such a case. Where else could you find
a town built so compactly that its citizens lived cheek to jowl in
many three-story tenements? Yet, a town which by population
could qualify as a city but chose to remain a town, meeting each
Winter at Annual Town Meeting to appropriate the taxes necessary
to run first class schools, a quality public safety program, and
provide health care for the underprivileged.

Clinton had its share of quirky qualities as well. Whereas the
dozen or more towns across America that shared Clinton's name,
all named after De Witt Clinton, the early nineteenth century
American statesman, Clinton, Massachusetts, started as the
Clintonville village of Mother Town Lancaster, named by an early
industrialist for the luxurious hotel he stayed in on a trip to New
York City. In 1850 it gained sufficient fiscal autonomy to break
away and soon overshadow Lancaster as an attractive destination
for immigrating mill workers from much of Europe.

The great dam, built at the turn of the century, flooded almost half of its buildable land, thus making it an urban environment. Built on four hills: Cedar, Burditt, Greely, and the Acre, Clinton took on many of the aspects of urban ghettoization as succeeding waves of immigrants sought housing with their kinfolk and built worship places within the clearly demarked neighborhoods.

As the anonymous poet concluded, the testing came with the Great Depression and the loss of livelihood to thousands of factory workers. But emerging from the Second World War there was a new sense of confidence and optimism, underwritten by Clinton's unique ability to develop friends in high places, politicians and presidents.

ethnicity

Beyond and even within my neighborhood in Clinton there was a consciousness of boundaries. The Irish – not my Ulster Irish, but the West of Ireland Irish – made firm claim of ascendancy before I came along. The high school football team was called the Galloping Gaels although the Browchuks, Stukas, Kamatarises, Mosas, and Williamsons were stars and they too suited up in Green and Gold. Turner Hall in Germantown nurtured the art of gymnastics. On the frozen Nashua, each winter it was the burly Poles from Green Street who dominated the ice hockey games.

The Polish and Italian girls were much more interesting than the repressed colleens. Our first Polish words were used to taunt the budding adolescent Polish girls. Euphonically we called out (although to this day I have never learned to write it) "Yachtem veechy poka chami," which we understood to be making not too subtle remark as to how their breasts were fitting their training bras.

But despite the free and easy adolescent interplay there was an abiding sense that we each had a place. No young Italian Romeo would be welcome to go calling on the early English families on Cedar Hill. Italians would find priests of their tradition at Our Lady of Holy Rosary; Polish Catholics at Our Lady of Jasna Gora, while those of Irish Ascendancy worshipped at and controlled the Cardinal Church of St. John the Baptist which rated a Monsignor as Pastor.

Just down the street from St. John's was the turreted Church of St. Nicholas, where the growing Greek community had its reputedly interminable Sunday Eucharist. Greeks boys, much like Jewish boys, were inclined to sow their wild oats outside their ethnic communities before settling on what appeared to outsiders as an arranged marriage within the community.

The savagery and displacement of World War II brought yet another trickle of immigration to Clinton – those victims of genocide and the Holocaust. Even on East Street Extension we gained a Kinosian family, who were driven out of Armenia first by the Turks and then the Russians. Mr. Kinosian soon had his own photography studio going. My mother quickly bonded with Mrs. Kinosian who became a close friend until the end of their lives. Sons Nubar and Victor soon took a liking to American baseball and were soon hitting the long ball into Mr. Bousquet's garage windows. The Jewish Community sponsored a distinguished Viennese physician, Dr. Harry Poras and his heavily cultured wife Marietta, driven out by Hitler's Anschluss – settled at the foot of Cedar Hill and soon had a thriving practice going made up of patients from all the various segments of this amazingly diverse neighborhood.

Clinton proved once again for the Porases and for the Kinosians that they had a place where they would find friends and support and the future held great promise for their children. Son Nubar was a natural politician in this intensely political town – becoming the protégé of Fitchberg's Senator Joe Ward. He eventually wound up as the most popular sergeant of arms in the General Court. The Porases spawned a dentist from among their children who opened a practice next to that of his physician father. When Dr. Poras died, he left behind an active and involved widow who, now nearly ninety, cuts a strong, controversial figure on the Lancaster Board of Health.

pols and pres

Politics was in the water in Clinton. David I. Walsh, the first
Catholic governor of, and then controversial US Senator from
Massachusetts, was one of ours. His sister was the principal of
Parkhurst, my primary school, retiring just before my entry, but
still alert and lively. She survived the death of her controversial
brother, and at the end of World War II she was given the honor of
christening the new aircraft carrier, the USS Wasp. This was the
last carrier built in the Boston Navy Yards and much of Clinton's
citizenry were there as honored guests.

Not controversial in Clinton, but certainly on the national
scene, as chairman of the Senate Naval Committee, Walsh almost
single-handedly brought about the defeat of FDR's Lend Lease
Destroyers for Britain program. None of this bothered the minds
of the average local Irish Democratic pols.

Of course, Britain was held as equal a threat to democracy as
was Nazi Germany. Just like Joe Kennedy, then Ambassador to the
Court of St. James, Walsh believed we had no role to play in
Europe's wars. This came vividly to my mind while in my first
year at Clinton High during a modern history course taught by a
gifted teacher, Bob Murphy. "You should consider subscribing to
a weekly news magazine," suggested Bob. "There are two: Time
and Newsweek. But you should know that Time called our beloved
Senator Walsh a bumbling isolationist." Needless to say I subscribed
to Time.

Not only in the Senate, but also in the US House of
Representatives, Clinton was represented far more strongly than
would make sense for a town of 13,000 people. Joseph Casey,
quite contrary to Walsh, was a close ally to Roosevelt and his entire

program. He married a Wellesley graduate and moved out of small town politics into the big time. The Massachusetts Democratic Party nominated him to run against Woodrow Wilson's old nemesis, the senior Henry Cabot Lodge. Casey lost and soon became a lobbyist in Washington, only to run afoul of the law in the post war RFC scandal for which he served a time in Federal prison.

The remarkable and almost immortal Congressman, Phillip J. Philbin, second-string guard on the last Harvard football team to play in the Rose Bowl, followed Casey in the House. He parleyed this into a law degree from Columbia and founded a Philbin dynasty, which carries weight in the town to this day.

Indeed as I will relate elsewhere, it was Phil Philbin who was instrumental in my getting a scholarship to Harvard and I remained close to him when his role of vice chair of the House Armed Services Committee made him an easy target for the peaceniks of the seventies. Bruited about Clinton, also in my youth, was Jim Donovan, the New York City pol who unseated Vito Marcantonio, as a Manhattan Congressman, also had Clinton roots. Not bad for a small town! So politics came quite naturally to my youthful consciousness.

Some of this political history was from revived and embellished memories related to me over the years by my mother. So it was quite likely that at age four, FDR passed through Clinton on his way to his son's graduation from Groton School. Did I really get a chance to shake his hand as he sat in his open car passing Bigelow Free Library? Surely it was true that when US Postmaster General, Jim Farley came to Clinton on September 25, 1937 to personally dedicate the new post office, my mother in her confident manner had seated the two of us on the soon to-be-laid cornerstone and we had to be entreated to leave our perch so that with trowel in hand Jim Farley could cement the cornerstone in place.

Post Office Cornerstone

Building local post offices was, of course, central to the New Deal. Its impact was felt in Clinton in many ways. Born after the upturn from the Great Depression, I was early on conscious of its persisting social dislocations. My father, always the aspiring independent businessman somehow scratched out a living peddling his Raleigh products door-to-door to his fellow Ulstermen. He viewed with scorn his neighboring brother-in-law, David Brown, who worked for the Public Works Administration as it upgraded Clinton's water supply in the nearby Weekepekee Resovoir.

Two poignant memories of the still prevailing despair were imprinted in my young mind. Although my mother later denied ever having been there, I remember accompanying her to a welfare food outlet in one of Water Street's abandoned mills. As we stood in line to check out with our groceries, the woman in front of us dropped a brown bag spilling milled rice all over the floor. The woman burst into tears and on her hands and knees tried to brush as much of the rice as possible back into her bag. On another occasion, when I was with my mother in Worcester's Woolsworth's store, two police officers were escorting an elderly man out in handcuffs. My mother gently explained that the poor man, having nothing to his name, had tried to shoplift some cookies. That man was also in tears. Those times brought many tears. But, since we were of proud, Ulster Protestant stock, we would accept no handouts.

But growing up Protestant in Clinton carried with it a political identity of being Republican. Already there was some breakout of non-Irish Catholic folks. William Constantino had been elected State Representative and was indeed soon to appear on the Republican ballot as a candidate for State Treasurer. Walter Stuka and others from the Polish Catholic community registered as Republicans to improve their chances for a political career. But Protestants showed no signs of reciprocity. To be Protestant was to be Republican. So it was as the 1940 national election approached that all my kith and kin adopted the slogan "Win With Wilkie." But the prevalent mood in still isolationist Democratic Clinton was that "Roosevelt Kept Us Out of War" and the nasty rhyme heard on High Street was:

> **"Roosevelt's in the White House Ready to be Elected/**
> **Wilkie's in the Garbage Heap, Ready to be collected!"**

What could we insipient primary school Republicans to do about this? Across the street, our neighbor Malcolm McLeod had a great idea. We heard on the radio news that Wilkie would be speaking in Worcester in September 1940 and would be passing on to Lowell for his next speech going right past Clinton's Boston and Maine Railroad Station. Malcolm and I formulated a plan. We'd make Wilkie's train stop.

So a half hour or so before Wilkie's expected arrival off we went to the railroad station. A line of baggage wagons as usual stood on the northbound platform. He grabbed the front handle and pulled and steered. I got behind and pushed. The station manager spotted us and shouted, "Hey, you kids!" He grabbed us and our mothers were then summoned to collect us. So that was how FDR beat Wilkie in 1940 and it was not until 1952 when Harry Truman came and actually stopped at that station with his appointment secretary Clintonian, Matthew Connolly, that I made my next partisan appearance in that venue. But that is another story for another time.

CHAPTER 2
STARTING OUT

Carter Memorial Hospital
Gordon Graham born March 18, 1934

genesis

Life lived forward can only be understood looking backward. Yet whoever wrote that caption beside my photo in the CHS '51 yearbook –

"life is but a jest and all things show it."
I thought so once myself but now I know it"

– captured who I was then and indeed now looking back over these fifty years, I can't imagine a better retrospective on a now largely lived life. As I "sailed through life with nary a care" I pause only with cheer and gratitude to mark those events and those people and the many, diverse places which together made my life "careless."

Ironically, of course, it was the certitude of ready care from the beginning, which inspirited the emerging me. Lillian Cumming and George Graham had no Dr. Spock in their day to instruct them in parenting. Indeed for almost ten years from their marriage they had all but given up hope of conceiving a child. So they turned to providing foster care, taking on a whole family of "state children" as the government's foster care program was known as in those days. That family was the Samples: Jesse, Eddie, Helen and Elaine. When my mother Lillian finally conceived in her 40th year, I was delivered in Clinton's Carter Memorial Hospital and brought home to the four-bedroom house my father had built for my mother in 1925. Built as a twin of the Free Methodist parsonage, it stood overlooking it to the south at the end of East Street Extension. The Free Methodist Church, housing a tiny community which my father had helped establish and which previously met in the "Item Offices," had also been built on the lot to the West of our house, facing High Street. High Street was the northerly extension of "the main drag" Route 110, the major artery running from the Middlesex mill towns of Lowell, Lawrence and Haverhill south to Worcester, known in the United States as "the Heart of the Commonwealth."

Born during what I was told was a mid-March blizzard, I was wrapped warmly and bundled into my father's Raleigh products car and brought home as the youngest member of what had previously been an entire foster family. Vague recollections are that Elaine and Helen Samples continued to live with my family, but Jesse and Eddie, already in their teens, had moved elsewhere.

As I grew up to primary school days I was regaled with stories from Helen Samples who came to live with us again before her marriage to the "rich Mr. Harrington of Princeton." Helen loved to scare me with stories about how she and Elaine would send my baby carriage plummeting down the steepest hills in Woodlawn Cemetery and laughingly delay to see how long they dare let it go before they chased after it. Not a confidence builder for childhood security, but somehow I never doubted the underlying love of my simple pietistic parents and the love of cousins and strangers who surrounded me in those formative years – lots of laughs and jest galore.

It was in Washington's Union Station as I was bidding my mother and father good-bye as they boarded the express to Boston that my father, then close to seventy, shared with me the specifics of my origins. "I sometimes think," he said, "that I can name the time and place of your conception. The last time your mother and I were on a train, it was a Pullman coming back from the Free Methodist Conference in Wilkes-Barre, Pennsylvania." So there it was. While others may have been conceived in sin, not so with George Gordon Graham. In utter Grace, it was coming back from a Free Methodist Conference.

roots

"Give me your tired, your poor,
Your huddled masses yearning to breathe free,
The wretched refuse of your teeming shore.
Send these, the homeless, tempest tossed to me,
I lift my lamp beside the golden door!"

Emma Lazarus 1849-1887

We the CHS Class of '51 sang these famous words shakily, some
more meaningfully than others. The hymn, arranged to the poem
carved on New York harbor's Statue of Liberty meant much to
some of us. More upbeat and inclusive to that majority who had
been born as first generation Americans was FDR's confrontational
greeting to the DAR after they refused use of their Constitution
Hall to Afro American soprano Marian Anderson. "Fellow
Immigrants" intoned Roosevelt, putting us all together as
newcomers to this ancient continent.

The legend we grew up with in Clinton was that the first
major wave of immigration was during the construction of the
Clinton Dam at the turn of the century – in its day the largest
man-made dam in the world. However, more than just the unskilled
mill hands of Clintonville were needed, so recruiters were sent
across much of Europe. From Germany were recruited teamsters:
stern Lutherans from Prussia and more liberal non-conformists
who established their own place of worship as the German
Congregational Church in what became Germantown. Recruitment
ties of family connections brought yet more Irish – like my father
George from County Down and my mother Lillian Cummings

from Mayo at Castlebar, but the largest contingent came from Louisburg, a few miles west of Castlebar. Most of the Irish worked construction, with the more literate moving quickly into foremen positions. From Italy came stonemasons, settling along Grove and Pleasant Streets in what would become "California". A large contingent of Polish laborers settled down the valley from the proposed dam structure, along what was to become Green Street. Ethnic boundaries and neighborhoods were well established before my parents arrived. Up on the hill – Cedar Hill – overlooking all these new neighborhoods were the homes of the Coulters, the Stevenses, the Jaquiths, mostly of WASP lineage, long endued with a community sense of noblesse oblige, who still ran government, the banks and endowed the Episcopal Church of the Good Shepherd and the First Unitarian Church, providing acts of charity and good works to both early and late arrivals.

My maternal grandfather, John Gordon Cumming – from whom my second name came – I knew fairly little about, except that his gravestone in Cumming lot in Woodlawn Cemetery bore the inscription "Born in Scotland." He was listed as a "pensioner" according to county records of his children's school registrations and sometimes his name was spelled with an "s" on the end. Recently, just before the turn of the 20th century into the 21st, in my pre-ordination field work in the Church of Ireland I was able to document more about that bit of family history. Now on a shelf in the "Protestant School" in Westport, Ireland, are the dusty old attendance ledgers of the early 20th Century. There is recorded the starting and ending dates of all six of John Gordon and Ellen Harrison Cumming.

Lillian Cumming, my mother, was one of six daughters and two sons of Ellen Harrison Cummings and John Gordon Cummings, all born and raised through Church of Ireland Grammar School, before immigrating as an entire family in 1909-10. John Gordon had been born in a tiny village in the northeastern-most county of Banff, Scotland in 1841. In his youth he had joined up with the British Imperial military serving in West Yorkshire's

West Riding regiment, posted in turn to Egypt, India and finally to Castlebar Barracks, County Mayo, Ireland. Although never holding a rank higher than private, he was part of a cadre of regimental "school teachers" who brought some minimal measure of literacy to Her Majesty's Forces.

Sometime shortly before 1880, perhaps on home leave with his regiment, John Gordon met Ellen Harrison from Leeds, England, and induced her to follow him to his Irish posting where they were married and began raising a family soon thereafter. The boys Charles and Thomas entered the parish school at age 7 and from 1886 on, Thomas, the second oldest, actually put in 14 full years of schooling before he withdrew in 1900. Charles also managed nine years of education, while daughters Annie, Ellen, my mother Lily and her twin Janet (also known as Jennie) put in six or seven years before the family began immigrating around 1910. School records of the time do not reflect attendance by yet another sister Elizabeth (Doty) who also came to America and married Carl Wheeler of Lowell, spawning a quite separate but large branch off from the Cummings.

There is reason to believe that some of the boys the family returned to Midlands, England looking for work before leading the immigration to Massachusetts. But by 1910, the entire Cummings clan had moved on to Clinton, led by my grandparents who set up crowded quarters in the company houses in Clinton on Nelson Street.

They found employment in the Bigelow Carpet Mills on Nelson Street in Clinton, where the girls quickly picked up the elementary skills required to run a carpet loom. Charley became an apprentice plumber and Tommie began a checkered career, most commonly working as a sexton in the Protestant churches of the area.

Only in adulthood did I learn the dirty little secret of the male Cummings. Like their Catholic Irish cousins, they too, were to a man afflicted with alcoholism. Cousins, a decade or so older than I, began confiding that grandfather had never had a sober day in America. Twice a day, my mother, between minding her looms on Union Street, scurried over to the Old Timers Bar on Church Street and as dutiful daughter brought home a bucket of beer for granddad. This continued until his liver finally gave out after four years and he died. He was buried in the Orange Order's lot in Woodlawn Cemetery, soon to be joined by son Charley, the plumber, who while showing off his balancing act over the canal next to the Lancaster Mills, lost his footing and pulled down by the weight of the pipes sunk to the bottom and was beyond all help by the time the fire department could dredge him up. He, too, was buried an Orangeman, but later, with granddad, was dug and up and transplanted to the Cummings family lot purchased in 1936 when Grandma Ellen passed while my parents and I were on a homecoming visit to Graham relatives in Northern Ireland.

My mother and her sisters – Ellen being the marked exception – did manage lifelong marriages to hard-working men and although they themselves occasionally returned to the mills for the extra income, largely spent the rest of their days raising decent first generation Americans. But the blight of alcoholism lived on in almost all the males of the next generation and early on, I became aware of how difficult it was to keep under control. I will deal with the issue again when giving an account of the Graham side of the family, but it all goes back of course to the use of alcohol among the Irish, both there and wherever they have been dispersed throughout the world. Unlike people of Eastern or Southern Europe, Irish males tend to drink apart from family meals, in pubs or alone on binges.

If alcohol was the bane of the Cummings, irresponsible begetting of children was the Graham legacy. A recent review of my father's family going back just one generation managed to produce six aunts and seven uncles and at least one hundred first cousins.

Now every two years without apology or even self-consciousness, these cousins and their offspring gather near Worcester – together with their inbreeding cousins the McCulloughs – and celebrate this genetic recklessness.

My great-grandfather George – after whom my father and I were named—sired six sons and six daughters up in Ulster's Mourne Mountains. Clearly the Graham tribe, like the Cummings, started off as Lowland Scots, but since there is no memory of coming across the sea as settlers, they in likelihood were Irish born at least since 1700.

Marriage and christening records I have seen in County Down's Kilkeel Presbyterian Church tell a uniform story of male farmers and illiterate "home weaver" wives. Their lifestyle and religious belief system was clearly formed by the rock-scrabble Mourne Mountains from which they eked a subsistence living. My father's generation yearned to be independent shopkeepers and he did an apprenticeship in a Rathfriland hardware shop though nothing came from it when he immigrated to America in 1906.

It was left to the children of his youngest brother Francis, born when my father was already 22 years old, to become incredibly successful shopkeepers. But among my father's generation, there was that huge period of fecundity, cheerfully engaged in my grandfather Samuel and his illiterate and hapless wife Margaret, which doomed an entire generation to leave school early, try to find a patch of fertile land on which they could raise a few sheep or pigs, or simply respond to the siren of the New England textile recruiters and ship off to America.

The sequence and frequency of births in that little thatched roof cottage in the Mournes was staggering. My father, the oldest, was born in 1887, when his mother was twenty. Then followed another six sisters and seven brothers until when Uncle Francis was born (together with a stillborn twin) in 1909, Margaret had had enough and at age 42 went on to meet her Maker. Granddad Samuel, none the worse for wear, lived on in Francis' home down Church Hill from the Bronte family church, until in 1946, at age 87 he went on to rejoin Margaret where one hopes there is a world where we are not given in marriage or constant birthing.

The children of Samuel and Margaret split almost equally between those who immigrated and those who stayed. None did particularly well in Ulster or America. Uncles Samuel, William and Aunts Annie, Margaret, Lizzie, and Susan came to America, while Alexander (Sandy), James, Henry, Robert, Francis, and sisters Mary Jane and Aggie all remained in Ulster. Aggie followed the tradition of staying "at home" to look after the parents. But as a family, there remained a close bond. Letters from those who emigrated were sent back regularly and read assiduously by those who stayed behind. There is apparently a storehouse of such letters as the legacy of the last to die, Francis, and custody of these is with his son Samuel who is reluctant at this late stage to further share these important documents.

So in place of documents, we again go by the repeated oral history. The most recent one to reach me is that my father's journey to America in 1906, at age 19, had originally been booked on the Titanic out of Belfast. He is reputed to have arrived at the docks too late. If true, this obviously has considerable impact on my later emerging life. How close I came to not being!

Father George was not the first to arrive in Worcester County. His sister Margaret and her cousin and intended husband John McCullough (engaged to Maggie when she was 14) came to America separately but were married and moved to Worcester where Uncle John had begun a long career as an independent housepainter.

My father, a naive 19-year-old was met at the Boston docks by a couple of pool sharks that took my father to his first and last game of pool. Once there he was then induced to bet his entire savings. Thus, broke on arrival, he was crestfallen in seeing that Tremont Street was not indeed paved with gold. My father somehow contacted John and Maggie McCullough in Worcester who kindly sent carfare and soon my father was in Clinton, working as a loom fixer at Bigelow Carpet. There he met Lily Graham, a loom operator and a vibrant, much sought after young woman. Then followed almost twenty years of courtship, when finally in 1925, Lily saw the steadiness and persistence in George which she grew to value more than glamour. And so they were married that

May in the Free Methodist parsonage, the duplicate of the house that my father had built next door on East Street Extension, behind the tall brick church, which would encompass so much of all our lives, especially mine. With whatever persistence went into their desire for a family, nothing resulted in early issue and it was a full nine more years before I, their one and only son and heir, was born.

Throughout the Graham/McCullough tribe there persists to this day a stern disapproval of the outer world. Perhaps it is the Calvinist tradition of the elect somehow mixed in with a gender divide. The awkward and secretive use of alcohol is central. Outwardly, most of the men would assume abstentious postures. "Never tell your mother that I am offering you a drink ... never drink in a public restaurant or with a meal." At reunions the men would sneak away to the back shed or to the cellar and there share a pint bottle of whisky before rejoining the ladies. Only over time did I discover that almost all of my uncles and cousins drank.

My father was the exception. Indeed, after a brief flirtation with the Eugene Debs Socialists, he enrolled in the Prohibition Party and supported the "Great Experiment" throughout its duration. He was incapable of understanding how his brothers, nephews or nieces could take even a social drink. His lame attempts at humor tried to cover his unease. He would often sarcastically share a story of the passerby who noticed a drunk lying in the gutter then hurried into the nearest tavern to tell the proprietor that his sign had fallen down. Then he would awkwardly attempt to get others to see the humor in his stern moralist view.

In lieu of any comfortable socialization with his brothers and even fellow workers, my father turned instead to his claim of election of who would one day earn his heavenly crown. But my father's righteousness was clearly not malicious. He would willingly extend kindness to any stranger and to all the forlorn people who boarded in our East Street home. However, his moral constraint made him an impossible example for me, as his only son, to emulate. Regardless, I knew he loved me and I had every reason to love him.

boarders

As well as the Samples foster family mentioned earlier who offered a wider range of siblings for this only child, there were the boarders. Boarders, usually older men – bachelors, widowers and separated husbands became a helpful sort of income for both my parents and for the Browns next door. When Margaret Brown went off to college, her bedroom was let to a kindly 70-year-old man, David Lister. When the Samples children moved on, my mother also decided to take in boarders and so in turn, took as our first boarders, the Free Methodist District Superintendent, Adam Kress; a youngish bachelor minister, C. Elvin Olmstead, and finally poor hapless Ellsworth Soli, a work-mate of my father from the Blake Flashlight factory. Each, in his way, played roles as mentors in my young life.

David Lister was the grandfather who was otherwise absent from my life. I must have been six or seven when he came next door. He picked me up early as a companion for walks into the Woodruff Heights woods and up to Clinton's Coachlace and Mossy Pond. Often we went in the company of the Bateson's dog, Soki and Music, the communal mongrel bloodhound. Both had the nastiest of habits of tagging along just in case Mr. Lister took a crap in the woods, on which occasions they, probably otherwise deficient in nutrients would gobble up the excrement. This occasioned Mr. Lister sharing with me his entire philosophy of nature's magnificent balance. As he taught me how to bait an earthworm onto a hook to take hornpout out of Mossy Pond, he shared with me – as best a bachelor could – a wonderful and personal understanding on how human reproduction did and should take place.

Certainly he gave me some of the essentials accurately. It had a lot to do with fluid which came, on demand, from the male penis. I was told that, somehow, what I was led to understand was probably urine, was somehow directed into some female cavity and this was how roosters caused hens to lay eggs and that was also in some variant or other the process of how human babies were inserted and finally emerged from women's bellies.

The word "sex", to the best of my now recollection just was not used. However, one thing for sure, we men wanted to be sure the product of our ejected fluid would be like ourselves, boy babies. That, according to Mister Lister, which was what he was euphonically called, could be accomplished by just making sure that the male fluid overpowered the female fluid. So, from age seven, I was urged to save up my piss for the big day.

Adam Kress, who came to us from a pastorate in New Jersey, came with the stigma of worldliness that made him a constant foil for my father's primitiveness. But we surely knew what we were getting. In 1938 or 1939, we had attended a Free Methodist Conference in Newark where Rev. Kress was in charge. This was indeed my first foray into metropolitan New York worldliness and it stayed with me for life. I liked it from the beginning. While my father kept to the conference agenda, my mother managed to take herself and me to the Flushing Meadows World Fair. Recollections are still vivid. The impending war in Europe was manifest as the German exhibit was being dismantled and going back to the Fatherland. But America's futuristic exhibits dominated the scene. In the performance auditorium, we gasped as the M.C. sat on top of a stove, which had a fridge inside. An elementary television set demonstrated how picture as well as voice could be transmitted over distance. The forerunner to LA freeways was the testing ground for GM's exhibit of streamlined cars of the future.

My mother made sure we got into the backseat of one of those cars and off we sped through the spaghetti maze of freeways. That was the context in which we welcomed Adam Kress who took up new lodgings on East Street, as the newly appointed Free Methodist

New England Conference District Superintendent, the closest office that the Free Methodists had to bishops.

Adam Kress' efforts to broaden my father's understanding of the larger world, however, resulted in resentment and retrenchment. I recall that comment was passed at the dinner table as to the quantity of food my father consumed famished from an eight-hour shift in the factory. Kress broadened his definition of temperance – which to my father involved exclusively abstinence from alcohol – as perhaps meaning moderation in eating habits as well. He took his argument further by describing alcohol as a natural by-product in the human digestive system, suggesting that the six ears of corn just whomped down into my father's stomach would produce the abhorred alcohol right there in my father's ample gut. For a man raised on the slogan that lips that touched liquor would never touch his, this cut it. Kress arranged from then on to take his meals at a time other than the family dinner hour.

The Free Methodist Church and Parsonage of Clinton

Perhaps two years later a second Free Methodist pastor came to live with us. The Rev. C. Elvin (soon to be Rev. Dr. C. Elvin) Olmstead came to us as a bachelor in his early thirties, balding, shy, and gawky, from unexceptional lineage. His father was the editor and publisher of the Free Methodist Church's Light and Life Press, out of Winona Lake, Indiana. Elvin was well on the way to his Ph.D. from Yale and came to us largely to write his thesis and stand in on Sundays as preacher in our next-door church. The rectory had been rented out. Olmstead would not assume much by way of pastoral duties but could make it boarding with us at a nominal fee. While clearly a scholar far beyond Kress' pretensions, Olmstead entered the parish and our home determined to get along by going along. Both my mother and father accepted him with high respect and I was encouraged to learn what I could from this talented man.

Overall that was the way it worked. Now perhaps seven years old and with some command of English I expressed to Olmstead my curiosity about foreign languages, especially those languages in which the Bible was originally written. Olmstead willingly responded. Using Psalm 119 as his teaching text, he soon had me rattling off the Hebrew alphabet: aleph, bet, gimel, daleth – I recall to this day. Olmstead also had the first portable typewriter I had seen and in between his own daily typing on his Ph.D. thesis, he would bring the Smith Corona down to our kitchen table and I would cheerfully practice touch-typing. I can look back now over those years and rejoice in what was my first real exposure to serious scholarship. What evoked respect in our household was looked upon with suspicion in the larger blue-collar community of Clinton who had looked upon the Free Methodists generally as a strange unassimilated people and here they had a scholarly, shy, gawky pastor, in his thirties who did not even mix with his own people – and he was unmarried.

Sexual deviance was seldom, if ever, talked about in my youthful years in Clinton. Right up through high school, the worst term for a deviant was "sissy" and we all knew nothing, really, of what sissies did except they did not do it with girls. Perhaps the only deviance that was given a name was "Peeping Tom." Among "lace curtain" Irish, who seldom undressed, even as husband or wife, in each other's presence, there was this fear that some night, somehow, the curtains would not be properly drawn and nakedness – most emphatically female nakedness – would be there to be spied on by those people who were clearly if queerly drawn to see such things.

It was definitely a much more suspicious and condemnable a folly than your neighbor's wife in the rumble seat of a Chevy. So that was the word put out in town – that Olmstead guy down on East Street was a "Peeping Tom."

Nobody knew for sure who started the rumor, but my mother quickly locked onto those who were cheerfully spreading it. Her prime suspect, among them, was Johnnie Fitzgerald, the owner of the Jennie Gas Station at High and Water. Not a more representative anti-Protestant could be found in town. A consummate Irish Catholic partisan, founder and head honcho of the Hibernians, he would saddle up his white horse from his Clark Street ratcheted each St. Paddy's Day, replete with the shamrock festooned horse blanket. Then he would ride that horse right up to High and Church Street and into Brocklemen's Market just to show those Protestants that St. Paddy was for sure one of theirs – so there! Well, up went my mother to the Jennie Station and poor Johnnie never knew what hit him. Grabbing him by the ear, my mother walked him right up High Street to Union, around the corner to the Clinton Police Station and brought him right into the open office door of Chief Mickey Kelly. "Mr. Kelly" said my mother with all dignity and due respect, "Mr. Fitzgerald here wants to confess that it was he who was spreading false rumors about Rev. Olmstead. He is here to tell you that he has no basis for those rumors and that he's going to stop." Of course I heard this whole tale entirely from my mother who was not given to outright lying. But what I do know is that the rumors stopped and Olmstead left a year later to academia with few scars from his three-year stay at 40 East Street.

The last and by far the least of the boarders was Ellsworth Soli. Perhaps it was our need for a little extra money but more likely, it was pure pity that induced my father to invite the only fellow Blake worker less popular than himself to come stay with us. Ellsworth and his variously demented mother and sisters came from neighboring Bolton, farm hicks to a one, and even while attending the Free Methodist Church found themselves frozen out of any social milieu available in our community. Early on, I accompanied Ellsworth and his two sisters on a Sunday afternoon visit to the county mental hospital in Worcester where they visited their, on again off again, hospitalized mother. While I waited in the car, I watched, in those days before psychotropic drugs, dozens of inmates hanging at the bars of their open windows and wailing a solemn chorus of lament without friend or contact with the outside world. Ellsworth carried that history of family affliction heavily. Whenever his own odd behavior came under criticism he fell back on his only defense: "Well, that's your opinion," he would say hoping to end the conversation there.

I would like to recall that I was kind and understanding to Ellsworth. Indeed I was not. Whenever he locked himself in our front bedroom, I would accumulate a couple of days of newspapers and light them to smoke him out. I was embarrassed in front of my friends that such an oddball lived in our house. I took special umbrage that his pride and joy was a 1940 four door Chevy, two years newer than my father's '38 Ford. So what to do? Ellsworth surely drew the pyromaniac out of my psyche. One morning I opened the gas tank of his car and dropped a gas soaked rag into the tank. A few flames shot up and I suppose I should count myself fortunate that I was not immolated on the spot. Still when Ellsworth moved out before my 12th birthday I finally felt myself freed from the ignominy of the last and the least valued of my family's boarders.

Early on in my life, I was clear as to boundaries. Those seven houses on East Street Extension were the neighborhood. I still find discouraging that Clinton maps, printed for the 1950 Centennial, have no extension to East Street, south of Brook. But, we were surely there all along and we knew that ourselves. The permanent residents were two plumbers: George Hayter and George McLeod whose large lots took up the whole east side of the street, with the McLeod's field running right up to the New Haven railway tracks. On our side of the street, opposite to the McLeod field, working down toward Brook, was the Free Methodist parsonage, the twin to our house, which abutted its north side. Next, there was the slightly more elegant Browns' house, Uncle David, Aunt Annie, and cousins Margaret and Marion. To their north were the three-story tenements: 46 and 48 East Street, whose flats were, in turn, occupied, some for the short term and some for the long, by young newly arrived families and those older couples whose lives were becoming more modest.

Along Brook Street, up to Forest, and over on the High Street blocks were strangers who might be worth getting to know. But across those tracks lived the "Enemy." We shared little with them but gradually got to know the names of the boys. The girls would enter our lives in puberty but that is a different tale. Those boys, Paul "Cig" Joyce, George "Boozho" Thompson, Zeke Seymour, and the slightly older Dave Patterson were defined as hostile.

As World War II hostilities entered our fantasy lives and air rifles and aluminum helmets appeared in JCPenney and Aubuhon's, we made ready for battle. Our manpower was impressive, what, with the four McLeod boys, all within a three-year age range of me, and John Thomas Bateson and Nubar Kinosian, from the tenements.

Our assault weapons were readily at hand. The under-grading of the twin tracks of the New Haven was entirely composed of stones from a quarter to a half-inch in diameter. There were piles for the Enemy on their Pearl Street side and we readily collected our own missiles and stored them in a trench dug on the southerly side of McLeod's field. When the signal was given the seven of us would gather in the McLeod trench and hurl stones up onto Pearl Street where Cig, Boozho, and Zeke would hunker down in their rain runoff trench, awaiting the opportunity for counter attack. It is a wonder one of us didn't lose an eye or get at least badly bruised, but the railroad boundary held right up to the early forties.

The enemy had little occasion to cross the tracks. They had Shattraw's market as their convenience store and we had Hamilton's, soon to become Georgeson's, as our market on High Street. Most of the enemies were Catholics who attended St. John's Elementary School uptown. We all went further north to Parkhurst. Perhaps it was the devastating fire at Shattraw's in the early forties or it was the McLeods and me going uptown to school that brought about a truce by the end of World War II. But soon thereafter, good-natured rivalries replaced hostilities. Bousquet's Field, just south of the Free Methodist parsonage became the common rough-surfaced playground for football and "mushball" (a variant of

baseball played with a ball of string loosely wrapped with black
friction tape) to spare the windows of Bousquet's garage and the
parsonage, both of which abutted our playing fields. It remained
for our high school days as one community when "Boozho" and
"Cig" fast became my friends over a lifetime.

Boundaries did not serve only to exclude us from exposure to
others; they served to help us learn from each other – those six or
seven growing boys on East Street extension. In times before
television, we picked up our ideal of healthy boys from baseball
and boxing on the radio. We were either Red Sox or Boston Braves
fans. There was not a Yankee fan among us although we did hear
wonderful things about the Dodgers. We may not have fully taken
in that Joe Louis and Sugar Ray Robinson were Black, but we
knew that our guy Joe beat their guy Max Schmeling and we were
still rooting for him over Billy Conn, who was known as the Great
White Hope in the thirties.

So on slow summer days, we took to the street with only an
occasional car passing by and practiced our curve balls and drops.
Balls were tossed up on McLeod's garage roof and caught as looping
fly balls. In the mid fifties, Mr. McLeod built a basket hoop on the
back of the garage where there was no surface or room to dribble,
but on which we could practice our lay ups, our foul shots and
two handers, through the timeless game of O-U-T.

Then there was the birthday or was it with my paper route
money that I came by a set of four boxing gloves. Our boxing ring
was made of loosely strung ropes around two-by-four corner posts
next to the Parsonage. I would take on all comers and for a while
was the champ. But there came that anxious moment when I felled
Harry Spanier, a younger challenger from down Forest Street. Harry
fell and didn't get up. We brought cold water and finally brought
him to but that event scared me so that I chose to accept early
retirement as undefeated champion.

Then there were the trees and telephone poles upon which we
developed our practice of shinnying. The south end of East Street
was devoid of trees but there was a stark, many-wired pole across

from my house that had ladder prongs extending beginning about ten feet from ground level. Low enough for the telephone man from his truck to swing alongside and climb. But for us shorter guys, we needed to shinny – knees locked and pulling yourself up by your arms inch by inch until finally the first rung was reached. A maple tree between the McLeod and Hayter property was also ideal for shinnying. In those years before school or community sports we discovered within our boundaries ample opportunity to explore and test our young bodies, our ballgame and gymnastic skills to the point that when organized games started at uptown schools we were ready to compete with the best.

hurricane, 1938

Just what I was doing that afternoon of September 21, 1938 in Leon Dankiewicz's second floor apartment on Haskell Avenue, I have no recollection. I was just barely four years old but already aware of the street patterns of Clinton. I knew I was in the heart of Germantown, right next to the German Congregational Church – where sermons were still preached in German at that time. But the Dankiewiczes were surely Polish and there were few Poles in my young life. I suspect that Leon's mother had at some time worked in a mill with mine. They, too, were of modest blue-collar, immigrant stock and it seemed that was always good enough for my mother. No pretentiousness and you could be her friend. But, what is strange is that while Leon and I were of the same age and went through high school together, there were no further – or indeed previous – visits to each other's homes.

The Dankiewiczes, like us, had their Philco wireless in the living room and it was on most of that September afternoon. There was a big storm coming up the Coast from Florida and it was reported each and every hour. It might well turn out to sea, but if it turned inland, it would hit Central Massachusetts. The sun goes down around seven in September in Massachusetts, but there was a gray overcast that afternoon beginning at three. I can remember the ominous stillness mixed with an occasional breeze blowing the dried oak leaves up against the second story windows. However, for reasons I didn't understand we stayed right where we were and by nightfall, it was clear. We were in the eye of a hurricane and we were in for it!

As the wind picked up, more than leaves were in the air. We could see shingles ripped from the lower houses nearby and then a chimney came crashing down. It was just Mrs. Dankiewicz, Leon, my mother and me and as it got dark, we saw the lights first flicker and then go out altogether. Sometime late that night or early morning, someone, possibly my father, I can't remember, came with flashlights to get us. I have memories of walking down Church Street, through Central Park and seeing a huge oak having crashed into the classical Greek fountain – a replica of the fountain at the Philadelphia World Fair.

The Central Park Fountain

All around were men with flashlights guiding us, reassuring us that we would soon be home and thankfully, we were.

The blessing of East Street extension, at least at its southernmost extreme, was that we were without trees of any sort. Only years later did I learn that the devastation of Central Park and the loss of ancient oaks and maples totally transformed the residential tree lines of Clinton. Winds sometimes cresting at 115 miles an hour wiped out more than 2,000 shade trees and caused building damage exceeding $600,000, which can be put into perspective by noting that a good four-bedroom wood-frame house could still be purchased for $2,500. But in my 4-year-old memory, my one and only close contact with Leon Dankiewicz, later a distinguished Coast Guard officer, was that one night of anxiety in his Germantown home.

war comes to church

Pearl Harbor Day remains vivid in my memory. While there remains open debate as to whether FDR knew in advance of a Japanese attack, Clinton and most particularly, the Free Methodist Church was on war footing long before December 7, 1941. How could we not be aware? Much of the year's national debate had been taken up with Roosevelt's Lend Lease, a plan to "lend" escort destroyers for British supply convoys. Well, our Senator Walsh was FDR's chief adversary. With the earlier re-enactment of selective service, Fort Devens was already bustling with conscripts taking their basic training. For me, at 7 years old, the Free Methodist Church was the filter through which I would experience the oncoming war.

The McLeod boys and I would sit on the front steps of "my" church and watch the convoys of hundreds of two-and-one-half-ton trucks, interspersed every so often with jeeploads of MPs who would stop and hold back civilian traffic at intersections. On rare occasions, a company of light tanks would come rumbling by, causing such devastation to the pavement that it had to be dug up and the elaborate "macadamization" of state highway 110 begun.

Our little church community would soon find itself host to a diverse group of soldiers coming to Sunday worship. Many conscripts from the southern Bible Belt found our unworldly and fundamentalist tradition close to their own. A small community of Mennonites, as firm pacifists, did alternative service as medical assistants and the base hospital gently inserted itself into our community and was made welcome.

Names still stick with me – particularly those whose mark went well beyond that short pre war season. There were Louis Cappetti, Larry Corporal, Jimmy McManus, and George May.

Louis Cappetti, from the start, insisted on center stage. Characterizing himself as a converted ex-Catholic, he was showcased and soon given the pulpit. In our first encounter, we were left with memories of a devout, somewhat charismatic man. A man to be accepted and honored. Indeed, when the War ended in 1945, Cappetti returned with an Australian war bride and moved to not only re capture his Free Methodist role but also quickly took steps to set up his own little Pentecostal church. Chapatti first arrived to set the stage for his re-entry into Clinton and my parents joyously welcomed him and set him up in our front bedroom. At the time, I was sleeping in the "back bedroom" which could only be entered by passing through my parents' room.

Late one evening after we were all in bed, Louis called out my name and said he would like to see me. I quite naively left my room, passed through my parents' room and entered his. When I got there, he suggested that I get into bed beside him so that we "could have a good talk." My mother, quickly sensing what was going on, called to me and ordered me back to my own bed. I only had a dim sense that something strange had come close to happening.

Then Mabel, his war bride arrived, a hefty and hearty Australian woman in her mid thirties, given to wearing loose clothing and exuding a looseness to her whole being. They took a duplex house down on Main Street near where Louis rented a storefront for his church and soon the rumors began. Besides the free will offering that Louis was receiving from his little flock each Sunday, Mabel also, by her free will or more likely under Louis' guidance was gathering an offering of her own. Soon word reached Chief Kelly and in the subtle but effective way of small town police, Louis and Mabel moved on to gain flocks in other pastures.

The only other soldier who did return at war's end was Jimmy McManus. Jim was a genial sort, though not sufficiently filled with holiness that he could ever quit his "Wings" cigarette habit. But at War's end he did at least come by and thank my mother and father for the warm hospitality they had shown a lonely soldier.

Larry Corporal is in my memory first as just an adjunct – a soldier who arrived with Cappetti. But soon after his arrival Cappetti alerted the community that Corporal had had some sort of breakdown and was in the base hospital. For some reason, my father took me along for a hospital visit to see Corporal. I have just a hazy memory of the barred and locked door in the hospital through which we could see hapless, raving soldiers, singing, chanting and showing all sorts of displays of mental instability. The wardens let my father in beyond the gate to see Corporal, who was reported to be "religiously insane." My father somehow took all this in stride, despite having experiences of being caught up involuntarily into ecstatic experience himself, he raised no objection to this diagnosis. We learned that Corporal was quickly thereafter discharged as unfit for military service.

George May was the only one we knew to be a war fatality. Although it could well be a later expanded fantasy, May was warmly received and entertained in the Brown family and had a friendship with Cousin Margaret which continued through correspondence when George's unit was dispatched for the invasion of the Philippines. Then word somehow reached Margaret that George had been killed in combat. For a woman, not particularly attractive and of an introverted nature, this became a consoling memory for the rest of her lifetime. George, we were assured had intended to return and marry her at war's end.

But, back to the beginning of my story. On Sunday, December 7, 1941, at least Chapatti and Corporal and possibly Jimmy McManus had returned after the eleven o'clock service at the Free Methodist Church. Central to church discipline, none of us listened to the radio on Sunday except perhaps to hear Charles Fuller's Old Time Revival Hour. That Sunday, however, word had spread. Something ominous was in the air. At one o'clock, the message came by way of a news bulletin. The naval forces of Japan had made a sneak attack on our fleet at Pearl Harbor. All military forces were immediately ordered to report to their stations. Quickly that little cadre of Free Methodist soldiers collected their caps and headed off to Fort Devens, leaving behind a strong memory of war's beginnings to this 7-year-old.

Pony Boy

cousins Pony Boy

What with six married uncles and three married aunts on my
father's side and one married uncle and three married aunts on my
mother's side – all committed to being fruitful and multiplying –
I was surrounded by first cousins! As an only child, I quickly
compared them to a heavenly host singing praises to the Lord sent
there to do battle for my cause. From the beginning, the girl cousins
championed my causes. At least four of them saw it as their duty
to introduce me to those aspects of life from which my parents

carefully guarded me. Thus, it was cousins Elsie and Grace who took me to my first movie and cousin Marion who showed me that more could be done on schooldays than showing up to school.

The Lowell cousins Florence and Betty Wheeler had a wild side which captivated me on our Thanksgiving visits. It was their older sister Ruth who was the one and only military model in WWII. Ruth, a registered nurse, enlisted immediately after graduating from nursing school in the Army Nurse Corps and we regularly followed her adventures in the European Theater. Dorothy Freeman, crippled by polio at age four, was the artistic one in the family. She took singing, piano and accordion lessons from an early age and would often be called upon to entertain us on our frequent visits to her tenement apartment in Worcester.

Worcester was also the home of those Graham cousins whose mother or father came to America in the early twentieth century. The girl cousins in Worcester were all close to my age, the cousins by Aunt Susan in Canada and even the girl cousins on my father's side left in Ulster were variously characterized as "sweet" on me. For generations back the Graham and McCullough clans, from Ireland's Mountains of Mourne, had inbred and interbred, always believing it safer to marry within the clan. It was my great good fortune that the girls involved were as good humored about the whole matter as was I and we just let the old folks have their fun.

The male cousins on both sides were more remote from my life. On my mother's side the curse of booze was visited on the second generation of Cummings. My mother's regular line in meeting any of them was, "let me smell your breath." Oddly enough on the Graham side, the only male cousins I had contact with were both named Bill. One was the son of Uncle William and the other the son of my favorite Uncle Sam and Aunt Edith. The latter Bill was a leap year baby, presumably born in 1932, and his quadrennial birthdays were made thus made much more festive. I still have memories, going back to 1940, of trying, with great mirth, blindfolded, to pin the tail on the donkey.

Uncle William's Bill was the lone male in a large household of sisters including older twins. At first he saw his Clinton cousin, being almost the same age, as the brother he never had. The denouement came when we were both 16 and, on a lark, I suggested that we go to a Billy Graham Evangelist Rally in Worcester's Auditorium. What better way to spoof the whole show than going there with another Billy Graham?

Unfortunately, cousin Bill had not had his full range of vaccinations against altar calls than had characterized my youth. When the call came, off goes Bill along the sawdust trail to be prayed over by the deacons and then led off to the conference room to be farmed out to the evangelical church nearest him. Bill soon realized that his country cousin from Clinton was marching to a different drummer and we never again caught up.

For reasons I have never quite fathomed, the closest fraternal feeling I had to a cousin was my, then and even now, relationship with Cousin Jim, son of my Uncle James Graham, who never came to America. Jim, almost ten years my senior, began writing me letters when he, like so many Ulster men, avoided serving in the British World War II forces by seeking war factory work in England. Jim became an expert metal fabricator and for some reason when he was about twenty and I all but twelve, he began sending me monthly letters from England. We exchanged some quite serious cogitations on the role of our respective countries in the war, what it was to learn a trade and what must have been what his motive was in the first place, what it would be like to come live in America.

So it came as no surprise, when at war's end, Cousin Jim announced his intention of following the earlier immigration to America. He was sponsored by the first of the family immigrants, our common Uncle John McCullough and his cousin/wife Margaret Graham McCullough. The welcome mat was laid out. Uncle John procured a building lot right across Steele Street from the original homestead and they built a modern American bungalow for Jim. Then, again true to the family tradition, Jim looked not far afield for a bride and within a couple of years had won the hand of his

Uncle William's daughter Miriam. They married, settled in and soon raised a brood of children on their own. Jim brought with him, also, from Northern Ireland, a reinvigorated Orange Order identity. He, almost alone of his generation, brought with him the siege complex of the Protestant Ulsterman. And, while Uncle Sam and Aunt Edith as well as John and Maggie McCullough had kept the tradition alive even occasionally returning to the Olde Sodde to commemorate the Battle of the Boyne, Jim, alone of his and my generation proudly wears the Orange Sash. Quite recently he, in fact, visited me lamenting that at age 72 he found himself the youngest Orangeman in Massachusetts.

I have made occasional efforts to catalogue or at least count up those who are first cousins on both sides. Only a few of them have died so far and every two years on the Graham's side of the family, there is a gathering of clans in the Worcester area. The total of those whose lives have directly touched and influenced mine is surely more than twenty. But, cumulatively there are at least another fifty first cousins who somehow know of me and I of them. I am indeed surrounded by a heavenly host. For this I thank God and the fecundity of uncles and aunts galore.

CHAPTER 3
MY ELEMENTARY YEARS

Parkhurst School

primary terror

As I was escorted, by my mother the three blocks down High Street, to Parkhurst School to enroll in first grade, September 1939, it all seemed so safe and secure. The solid four-room brick building looked cheerful enough, although it did occur to me at the time that some confused educator had chosen to cram five grades into four rooms. But I was entering first grade at 5 1/2 and had some sense that most of the other kids were older and bigger. Still, I recall no anxiety as my mother brought me into Mrs. Tattersall's room and said good-bye and good luck. Yet, truly half of my classmates were clinging to moms and wailing their little lungs out. Soon all the mothers were gone and we were left with a stolid, stern, visaged schoolmarm who clearly had firm ideas as to how we were to behave and perform. Much of it was education by rote, repeated exercises of penmanship, reading, and memorization. I was soon at a loss in penmanship – the Palmer method having no place for left-handers. Mrs. Tattersall took a shot at switching me to right hand but soon gave up allowing me to point my nibbed ink pen away from me rather than over the shoulder in the approved method. Despite these petty embarrassments I found myself quite enjoying school and especially my new playmates. Play in primary school was a single gender activity. There was the boys' side and the girls' side of the play yard and the girls' basement and boys' basement when rain or snow required us to spend recess indoors.

Soon it became apparent that even some older kids were having problems both with learning skills and looking straightforward at Mrs. Tattersall for the full five hours of the school day. For these "misfits" there was a remedy. For those unable to stay up with the lessons, Mrs. Tattersall sternly constructed "dunce caps" a cone of paper, which was put on the sluggard's head and a high stool provided for the dunce to sit on while the rest of us learned our lessons. Somehow this was perceived as an effective way to help the miscreant catch up.

And a similar incentive involving peer pressure was introduced for those of us who were distracted or rowdy. The class as a whole was punished. Mrs. Tattersall would go to the closet she shared with her confederate and second grade teacher Miss Gillespie. She would tell Miss Gillespie, being certain that we could hear, that our behavior was such that we deserved to be locked in for the night and that she was going home and we would all spend the long, cold night alone unless repentance was received. The effect was predictable. Terror for many of the 6-year-olds! Heads would drop onto the desks and the tears would flow. Most of us put our heads down to avoid the condemnatory visage of Mrs. Tattersall. Somehow, from the beginning, I knew it was just a bluff so I would keep my head up and try to stare her down.

And it was this precociousness, I gather, that brought on the systematic brutality visited upon me by Mrs. Tattersall and Miss Gillespie for all of my five years of primary school. Obviously, this is something that over the years I would like to have forgotten. Now, on the eve of my 50th high school reunion I've canvassed other members of the Parkhurst class of 1939 and discovered in at least two other cases of ugly memories, which the individual wrongly attributed to something being wrong with them.

It was only three years later when I was promoted to fourth grade under Miss Sullivan – by everyone's estimate one peach of a teacher – that I got out from under this harassment. By then I had become close to a classmate, Jack Downing, now deceased, with whom I pondered many of the problems of growing up sensitive in a blue-collar, macho culture. I often visited Jack's home, then a modest upstairs tenement near Depot Square. His mother loved to put on the player piano and this was my first introduction to Chopin and Bach.

One day as Jack and I returned from our lunch, we walked together down High Street in a winter landscape of snow. For reasons that now escape me, there was a school rule that we were not to pick up snow on our way to or from school. Now, Jack and I had broached the rule in some simple way of pushing and shoving with Jack falling into a snowdrift. Suddenly from behind us appeared Tattersall and Gillespie. Tattersall inquired of Jack, "How did you get snow on your coat?" Protecting me, his friend, he acted surprised and said he didn't know – obviously not an acceptable answer. It immediately became an issue. The minute I got back to Miss Sullivan's room, a girl from Tattersall's room appeared saying that Mrs. Tattersall wanted to see me. I was sent down to her and in front of the entire class of first graders she announced that I would be required to stand there until I confessed to having broken a solemn school rule. For more than an hour, I stood there stoic and determined while the class work continued. At that time, my weakness was a nervous stomach. As two o'clock turned to 2:30, I felt it coming. "Mrs. Tattersall," I implored. "I am going to be sick. May I go to the basement?" "No," she responded, "you stay right there until you are ready to speak the truth." I let go over my shoes and went home that night stinking of vomit. When my mother got the story out of me, I assure you Mrs. Tattersall was about to meet her match. The next afternoon my mother took off from her job at the Colonial Press and went down to report the whole affair to Miss Glenn, who though the principal in title, was powerless to discipline a teacher whose appointment was made by a totally politicized school committee. But when my mother spoke of getting a lawyer, there was a back down. In honesty, I would acknowledge having taken the whole experience largely in stride, but over the years I have seen lives shrunken short of full development brought on by a couple of deeply disturbed teachers who should never have been given the great responsibility of nurturing children.

Corporal punishment in schools, and indeed in the homes of my classmates in the 1940s was the rule rather than the exception.

Indeed the ruler was used more commonly to whack knuckles than to measure length. "Spare the rod and spoil the child" was commonplace in my father's understanding of child rearing. But it was left most commonly to my mother to do the chastising and for this she kept a slender tree branch – a switch – over the kitchen stove. Rather than deliberate punishment for misdeeds, it was usually applied to break my spirit when I was tempted to contradict or answer back. Two or three applications to my bare legs was usually enough for me to yield and either concur or withdraw whatever dissent I had offered.

Graver punishments were left to my father with the words "wait till your father comes home." Little elaboration was conveyed as to my actual misdeeds, but my father was the loyal executor of my mother's verdicts. With no particular zeal, he would take down his razor strap and apply it with swift and powerful strokes to my back and bottom until I would beg him to stop. Yet, while he did it with determination, I have no memory of anger – just a necessary compliance with a scriptural injunction.

I was probably nine or ten when I faced down my father's punishments. My first recollection was standing up on my bed as he came toward me with the strap and telling him he wouldn't be getting away with this much longer, but that first time was only a standoff. On a later occasion when he came at me with the strap, I just ran out the door onto the driveway between our house and the parsonage. This was the first time I became aware of my father's advancing age and mortality. I ran and he chased. As I raced along the drive and up the embankment, he followed, tripped and fell heavily to the ground.

Suddenly, I felt sorry for him. I ran back to this crumpled, crestfallen, 55-year-old man and offered him my hand. I helped him to his feet, making sure he was all right, but then continued my flight. He had no spirit left to follow and as I recall, this was the last corporal punishment I ever received from my caring but hapless father.

long way home

School hours in Clinton's first seven grades were 8:25 A.M. until 3:15 P.M. with a whopping two hours off for lunch at midday. With most parents working factory shifts from seven to four, we kids found our way to and from school on our own – only in post war years with the assistance of some in-town bus systems. With my parents working straight through lunch, I learned early on how to fend for myself. For a year or two, I was given meal tickets at the local diners but mostly lunch came from opening a can of spaghetti or soup or making a sandwich.

Getting to Parkhurst School, for me, was a ten-minute walk with lots of free time to explore. Time to find longer ways home and the woods beckoned. At the north end of East Street there was a brush-strewn pathway down to the South Branch of the Nashua River, where quite handily a beaver dam of logs provided an easy passage over to Mamefka's Field on the Eastern floodplain. A few hundred yards north was the Wagon Trail up into Woodruff Heights, once a wonderful grove of mixed pine and hardwoods. For decades, they stood surrounding long abandoned cabin cellar holes, which once bracketed the old 19th century settlements. Though now long gone, a special place provoked mystery and fantasy into my young life.

At the top of the wood, the trail again turned southward, crossing the New Haven line just before the entrance to the siding track over which carloads of pigs were carried to Hoffmann's slaughterhouse. Down that sharp railway embankment over needle strewn pine groves down again to the bend of the Nashua, where marshes and swamps lined its solid embankments marking inlets and woodland springs. I treasure the memories of lying there on a fall day watching water spiders criss-crossing the surface, their path broken quite regularly by the heads of terrapins and green frogs in a balanced aquatic world. Along the east bank, all the way to High Bridge, there were stepping-stones that I took back to where I started. Climbing the embankment, I encountered dozens of holes, homes for the garter snakes, who when lazing in the midday sun could easily be scooped up and hidden in the garage, in a Crisco can. They were then saved for the auspicious occasion when someone dared to bring one right down to Parkhurst's fourth grade and drop it down the back of Barbara Burke's dress. This was on a clear spring and fall afternoon the only proper way to go home from school.

Winter was a bit more treacherous on the Southern Branch. Ice formed pretty solid just before Christmas allowing easy access to test those new skates. But, as the late January thaw came, you had to carefully choose the patch of ice used to cross the river. The older McLeod boys, while we were all still at Parkhurst, made a poor guess one late February afternoon. Since their grandmother Mrs. Wahl was always on hand in their house, they feared chastisement if they showed up drenched and frozen at home. My home was considered the safe house. So carefully circling around Brook Street up to High and in my back door, there they perched for the two hours it took for our coal stove oven to dry out their pants and underclothes. But in spring and summer, over the river and through the woods was the best way to come home from school.

movies – cowboys, shrinks and u-boats

The Strand Movie House

That first visit to the Strand Movie House was at age four. The movie was "Snow White and the Seven Dwarfs" and I was hooked! I still remember swinging down the gilded, mirrored lobby, hand in hand with my cousins, Elsie and Grace Cummings, who first had to persuade my mother that Snow White was not about deviant sex.

I loved the movies and I wanted more. So, beginning at age eleven I got my fill. Sometime in the early forties, another cinema opened on High Street, playing only on weekends and showing strictly Westerns. One double feature played Friday and Saturday and two new movies on Sunday. The Strand was every night with matinees on Saturday and Sunday and it was strictly new feature films – perhaps a week behind Worcester's Warner theatre openings.

The Globe Westerns created cult followings and we craved to know what our Cowboy heroes did in "real life." As I am writing this, the papers have just announced that Dale Evans, the 88-year-old widow of Roy Rogers, has died. We knew that Roy had a wife in real life, who often appeared in the same film. But Roy's kisses were reserved for his horse Trigger. To me, Roy Rogers was twice the man of Gene Autrey, even if his horse Champion actually danced when Gene played guitar. But, it was William "Hopalong Cassidy" Boyd whose celibacy we could be confident in. Maybe he was close buddies with George "Gabby" Hayes but in the old westerns there were very few girls to clutter up our affections.

Admission to either cinema was initially 10 cents for kids and 25 cents for adults. That made regular attendance easy. However, with the deepening of the War, excise taxes were added in 1942, bringing it up first to eleven, then twelve and finally a hefty 13 cents by War's end. This price increase was offset by scrap metal Saturday matinees, where admission was free for anyone appearing with a pound of iron or lead. Friendship with George McLeod, the plumber, was handy on those occasions. At 12:30, we would stop by his Church Street establishment, pick up a couple of pipe elbows and head back up High Street for a free Saturday afternoon double feature.

There were many double features in those days. I think I can safely claim to having seen every change of films in the Strand between the years 1944 and 1951. Some of them two times over and, at least one, I recall seeing four times: twice on Sunday and then Monday and Tuesday evenings before the Wednesday mid-week change. The feature was "Spellbound" starring Ingrid Bergman and Gregory Peck and its co-feature was "U-boat Captain" a remarkably propaganda-free film of German submarine warfare. But my lifetime fascination with Freudian psychoanalysis was fixed by "Spellbound." I have of course seen it on television since but those ski scenes with dreamlike trail patterns in the snow are now part of the interior furniture of my mind.

So a special thank-you, "Hopper" Kilcoyne, forever manager of the Strand, for providing the foundation of this lad's education.

pigeons and pets

From my earliest years, I was aware that my parents had no affection for animals, perhaps, in my father's case it was growing up on a subsistence farm where animals were used for food or for herding flocks. My mother's aversion seemed deeper. She recounted this story repeatedly so that I can now picture, in my imagination, exactly when her nursing me came to an abrupt halt the summer of 1932. She was nursing me on the screened front porch of 40 East Street when a cat that had found a home with the Samples foster family took a fit, rushed out onto the porch and scrambled up the screen right in front of us. It gave her such a fright that her breast quickly dried up and after that, I was put on the bottle. I don't remember feeling any fear, but Mother's anxiety with any household pets persisted through my childhood. Indeed, I don't believe I ever saw my father or mother ever pet or fondle an animal – or for that matter each other.

By the fourth grade, I was netting from my two paper routes more than six dollars a week and those dollars were burning a hole in my pocket. And, Billy Watson could spot one of Barnum's "suckers" every bit as surely as P.T. himself. Billy, whose house complete with chicken coop and large garden, was on both my way to and from school and his family subscribed to the Afternoon Gazette. Billy – without ever really sharing much of the rest of his boyhood life with me – got me interested in pigeons, a flock he kept in his garage next to the chicken coop. To this day I don't believe I have ever have seen an authorized book on pigeon breeds, but Billy taught me the basics. The main breeds were Pouters, Tumblers and the rare and highly valued "genuine homers" the latter discernible from park pigeons only by sophisticates like Billy.

Pouters, whose trick was wonderfully anthropomorphic, could puff themselves up by holding their breath in their breasts. Tumblers, with clear, bell markings on their backs, specialized in aerial acrobatics and homers, of course, could be depended upon, wherever taken away in their basket, to find their way home – home to their true owner presumably.

The price was right. One dollar-fifty for the tumblers, two for the pouter, and three for the homers. I learned early on somehow to live on that 25 cents a day my father laid out on the kitchen window sill so I readily accumulated what it would take to buy up Billy's entire flock. Regrettably, his Cub Scouting obligations required Billy to sacrifice his hobby, but I was deemed a satisfactory successor. First, though, I had to construct a coop of my own. The essentials were easy. Much of my father's stock arrived in large wooden crates through railway express. Since he had already made use of enough crates to provide off-floor shelving for his stock in our cellar, new crates were expendable and were well-suited to coop building. Just two adjoining crates would do it – one for roosting and the other for nesting. A wire "bob" served as the one-way entry to the roosting box so that release was under my control and the "homers" would assuredly just work their way through the bob knowing that I was now their owner.

Over the next few weeks, I purchased Billy's entire stock: two pouters, two tumblers and five homers – for a total of about $25. Indeed, I knew I was an authentic pigeon raiser as I watched the pouters pout, and on short trips, dependably returning by the next mealtime, my tumblers did their acrobatics on cue. But alas, there soon appeared a stray cat among my pigeons and over a week period, he/she gained ready access through the bob and indeed appeared to exit just as handily each time with a pouter or a tumbler greedily snatched in its jaws. The only evidence left was the lovely breast feathers from the pouters or the two toned back feathers from the tumblers.

But nothing would match my highly bred homers. I would let them out each evening – assuring them safety from the wily predator and in the morning they would return. But, one morning came – and no homers were to be seen. I took my concern to Billy and he was most sympathetic. Perhaps he could help me find some better homers. He would look around. Sure enough the very next week he had found a willing, if anonymous, supplier so I could restock on homers. In fact, there were four available at the earlier agreed price. Maybe I would have better luck this time. So down I went with my eight dollars. They looked every bit as convincing a homer profile as my earlier four. Indeed the markings were almost identical. But a deal is a deal. Of course, I was not totally dim and it dawned on me the third time around. After that, I eliminated the middleman and found all my future homers – distinguishable markings and all – right there among the flock eating my salted peanuts in Central Park.

However, it was Stubby, the cat and Fluffy, the dog who were my mainstay pets in primary school. After my mother's front porch fright with the fitful cat in our early nursing days, we, as a family, never sought out cats as pets. It was Stubby who sought us out – even before he/she became "Stubby." Though never an attractive cat but wonderfully appreciative from the start, "Stubby" appeared mewing at our front door and a saucer of milk would be set out under the front hedge. After that, Stubby became a regular – but still not yet as "Stubby." That appellation came about by a gross intervention of the New Haven RR Freight Division. Amidst the puffing steam engine and the whining of wheels on the gradual turn as the train departed for Boston, we discerned one night a clearly untrainlike screech and next morning we discovered the cause. There under our hedge was a badly battered yellow cat, his face a bloody mess and his never very distinguished yellow tail now attached only by a two-inch strip of fur-covered skin. I got my pocketknife and completed the amputation with only a soulful meeting of the eyes coming by way of reaction from the now definitely defined "Stubby." Somehow, that day she became family and we nursed her to some semblance of health. The impact of the train on her face had cracked the roof of her mouth and it was only with considerable effort that the saucer of milk provided daily for the next two years did not just dribble right back out her nose as soon as it was licked hungrily into her mouth. Though "Stubby" was never a promising contestant for the County Cat Show, he/she was a wonderful catalyst of accepting love.

Then there was Fluffy, my suicidal mongrel. I have no clear memory of how this mixed terrier entered our family life – but I have vivid memories of his exit! I was in the sixth grade and my mother was working the second shift, 2:00 P.M. to 11:00 P.M., at the Colonial Press bindery. Fluffy was from the beginning a nervous dog and, unlike most dogs at the time, was kept regularly on a leash. It was summer time and the Press had its own "Copper Kettle" lunchroom, open to the public, just across Chestnut Street from the Nashua River Municipal Beach. In order to keep some track of my summer time adventures, my mother often encouraged me to meet her on late summer afternoons at the Copper Kettle for a grilled cheese sandwich and milk.

That memorable summer day – a hot one which always seemed to set off nervous dogs – I brought Fluffy, on leash, down for a look at the swimmers at the beach with the thought of meeting my mother for a treat at her five o'clock break. We never got our treat that day.

As I took Fluffy onto the bridge over the Nashua, she panicked and pulled desperately trying to rid herself of collar and leash. I let go and Fluffy, collar, leash and all, raced across the street and into the main entrance of the Colonial Press. That was actually the last I ever saw of Fluffy. I did go into the offices near the door she entered and inquired as to whether they had seen an hysterical dog. Some said they had but that it had just raced by.

Only at eleven that night, when my mother came home from work did I learn the sad story of Fluffy's end. It seems that she had raced right across the factory floor, trailing her leash and jumped out an open window. The workers had seen all this but were just happy to be rid of this wild animal, so they returned to their routine of printing Good Housekeeping Cookbooks. Only when the night shift was leaving did someone notice Fluffy – still alive but barely kicking – hanging by her leash from the factory window. Some kind man went inside and cut the leash. To the amazement of everyone, Fluffy hit the ground running and raced about the twenty yards to the industrial bypass canal where Fluffy, without hesitation just jumped in, surrendered and drowned. Someone who recognized the dog relayed the story to my mother who then came home to tell me. I do not remember crying, just a feeling of stunned disbelief. My mother felt obliged to add the postscript. "You know," she said. "That is the same canal your Uncle Charley drowned in twenty years ago." Human suicide has only occasionally touched my life since. But whenever it has, it brings up memories of that hot August afternoon when I lost Fluffy.

daily news

Although my father, the religious fundamentalist, was no admirer of Harry Emerson Fosdick, the modernist, he would surely have agreed with Fosdick's remark that "one should look at the world with the Bible in one hand and a good daily newspaper in the other." My father, with his three years of formal education, woke every morning before five to read his Bible, and so he went from Genesis to Revelation, on an annual cycle, like clockwork. Having finished his scripture and his prayers, he would then turn to the Worcester Daily Telegram and read it almost cover to cover. Indeed one of the few worldly indulgences he allowed himself was a full daily perusal of the full page of Telegram comics, dwelling particularly on the realistic strips such as Gasoline Alley and Andy Gump.

I fell easily in line with this practice from fourth grade on. In the fourth grade, Eddie McCracken, now leaving Parkhurst School for Corcoran, passed on to me his Telegram paper route of thirty regulars down into the North End of town. Each morning, before six I would make my way up to the Telegram offices, often encountering the paper's manager, Guy Cutter, sleeping off a bad hangover. Since I took on the route in 1943, I would start my day by reading in detail the progress of the War. I have vivid memories of the start of the Africa campaign by Generals Patton and Montgomery and the D-day landings at the Normandy Beaches. Later when I also took on an Evening Gazette route, I followed the South Pacific campaign, through the dispatches of Ernie Pyle. His articles, giving form and structure to the V-mail letters I was receiving directly by that time from Jesse and Eddie Samples, formerly foster children in our household but now slogging through the jungles of Okinawa and Iwo Jima with the United States Marine Corps.

The paper also featured political columnists who tried to make strategic sense of that complex war. This was usually from a quite conservative and implicitly anticommunist stance. Recently, I discovered in the family Bible an essay I wrote for Miss Broderick my sixth-grade teacher on the occasion of V-E Day in early 1945 and my political bias already was there: "The forces of Nazi Germany," I reported, "had surrendered to the Allies *plus the Soviet Union.*" Already I was anticipating the onset of a new "cold war" where the Soviets would not be our allies.

The Telegram also carried other interesting columns on such things as etiquette and practical psychology. The latter was in a daily column, "Let's Explore Your Mind," where I began learning the challenge to look beyond the boundaries of daily life and try the unusual. One of the earliest experiences I tried suggested by that column was to visit the neighborhood diner at three in the morning for a rare exposure to those people who lived and worked all night. From those days to this, my day does not start properly until I have made my way through a good daily newspaper.

riding the rails

Growing up within fifty yards of a major rail line brought steam engines and rumbling boxcars into my early life. The rumblings left cracks in the living room ceiling that needed replastering every five years. But, there was a sense of early romance to those trains that passed by with the insignia on boxcars and cattle cars calling forth far away places. Chesapeake and Ohio, Northern Pacific, the Atchison, Topeka and the Sante Fe, were indelibly inscribed in my mind from the first day I could read. The siding next to the water barn is where the Ringling Bros. Circus parked its menagerie of animals, complete with roaring lions that disturbed this 5-year-old's sleep. With the coming of the war, a new sight became common – flatcars laden with heavy tanks in transit from Fort Devens to Boston Harbor for transport to England. All are a part of my early memories.

Familiarity quickly took away the sense of danger which parents tried to instill in us. Early on, we placed rocks on the rails hoping for at least a minor derailment. The signal caps placed on the mainline to signal passage of trains, we would detach and try to explode with hammers. Caps and rocks weren't the only things to be found on the tracks. Animals, wild and domestic, were often crushed under the powerful steel wheels. There was also one occasion when except for my precipitous action, Mr. Kelly from down East Street would have been crushed.

There were two Kelly Brothers down the street, beyond Brook. There was the sober hard-working Mr. Kelly and there was the hard-drinking Mr. Kelly, whom we boys would often taunt with "Old Mr.Kelly, with the pimple on his. belly." But there was one summer evening, as I watched the nine o'clock freight being assembled on the sidetrack and I caught a glimpse of what looked like a bag of clothes. I came closer and there was Mr. Kelly collapsed right next to the switch box. He reeked of beer and I was alone and he looked very heavy. But the train would soon be ready to move down the track. I thought of calling for help but time was short, so I tugged him by the shoulders, got him clear of the tracks and was thanked by mumbled curses. There were no hero prizes then for saving Old Mister Kelly with the pimple on his belly.

Something that stood out as an early challenge, particularly as freight trains were slowly and methodically assembled right up there on the sidings, was to catch hold of the ladders on the slowly passing boxcars and ride along at least for a few hundred feet before the train picked up speed. Then for the more adventuresome, there was the challenge of mounting the ladders up to the planks along the roof, walking the length of one car and then leaping over the gap over to the next walkway.

By age nine, I was among the leading daredevils, hanging onto the moving freight as it picked up speed in its eastward journey and leaping off just before it crossed High Bridge. That was on the New Haven line. Intersecting the New Haven at the Clinton Depot was the Boston and Maine Track, the mainline between Worcester and Portland Maine, which carried freight and passenger trains. Passenger trains were clearly closely monitored by conductors but the 60 car freights were staffed only at the front engine and in the caboose. These were ideal for longer rides, particularly southward over the stretch that ran between Coachlace and Mossy Ponds, right across South Meadow Road and off into the neighboring town of Sterling to our favorite destination, Balls Landing Rowboat Rental at Washacum Pond.

I recall doing this only two or three times since there were few takers and high risks. Catching hold of the train at Coachlace was pretty tame stuff. The train was moving at perhaps fifteen miles an hour until it passed South Meadow. Then it quickly picked up speed as it entered Sterling with the next crossing being at Balls Landing. I recall coaching Al Cooperman on the necessary technique. You run along next to the train before jumping aboard, I explained. It was getting off at high speed that was the more difficult trick. Be sure to hit the roadbed running or you're in trouble. Hopping off a speeding train running was more easily said than done. Sure enough, as I gave the signal upon approaching Ball's Landing, the train was doing more than forty. I jumped first and managed to stay on my feet, but poor Al was not so lucky. He hit the cinder bed backwards, fell flat and rolled over a couple of times, before finally righting himself. He was covered with huge scratches on his legs and arms. It was not the best way to start a day of boating from Ball's Landing.

Mama's Boy

mama's adventure

Obviously, I have always had a sense of adventure and I'm sure it didn't come from my repressed, foreboding father. No, it was from the Cummings side, I'm sure because so many of the cousins on that side also shared my sense of fun and danger. Although my mother could appear anxious at the most conventional of situations, she, too, could readily rise to a challenge.

When I was about eight, there appeared as neighbors, in the parsonage next door, a most unlikely twosome: a female Free Methodist minister named Grace and her ageing mother. Grace was an aberration in clerical circles altogether and a bit of fresh air to free Methodism in particular. My mother, although fifteen years her senior, bonded immediately with Grace's adventurous spirit.

One day I excitedly shared with my mother that I had gone out to Bolton Airport and for just $10 had gotten to take a one-hour aerial tour of Clinton from a Piper Club monoplane. Mother thought "Why not Grace and me?" She rose to the occasion and over to the parsonage she went with her dare. Sure enough, Grace was game and off we went in Grace's car, the three miles to the airport.

"No Piper Cubs available for tours today, ladies," said the manager. "But we do have this open biplane, if you're up to it." Without a moment's hesitation from either of them, on went the leather helmets and the goggles and they raced out to the tarmac where they hopped into the front open cockpit with the pilot behind. The engine roared and off they went into the wild blue.

A half-hour later, two rosy-cheeked women debarked, full of pride and accomplishment. To this date, I think of my mother and Grace as pioneers of feminism.

first love

Even at ten, I knew the Stoddards ran Worcester. I had been delivering the Telegram and Gazette since I was eight and together with the Booth family, they dominated the masthead. Anita Stoddard was from Worcester all right, but not from that Stoddard family at all. She had, somehow, been discovered by the Clinton Free Methodists and had connections in Worcester. She was from Thomas Street, a street that is no more having fallen victim to redevelopment in the slum clearances of the sixties. In those days though, it was a narrow street running parallel to downtown Main Street and ending in the scrap yards of Morgan Machinery works.

Can I really now reconstruct what she looked like? Not easily. Anita was soft and unformed, straggly hair and the beginnings of budding breasts. She was willowy, but not as tall as me, although she was surely the same age or older. She had a way of looking at me that was soft and inviting and that was all I needed at ten. Life on Clinton's East Street had been a life of separation between boys and girls until then and Anita held herself apart from the Clinton and Seekonk girls, the former all too familiar from Sunday School days and the latter, of mixed Black and Indian heritage, a bit too exotic for this 10-year-old.

She had been offered a free 10-day at the annual Palmer Camp Meeting, so it just naturally happened. Anita just became my girlfriend and we sat together in the dining halls and walked together back and forward to the tabernacle and the interminable revival and testimony meetings. Had it not been for me, I am certain, Anita would have been saved that summer. But I, in my already cynical manner, offered her protection and a place where she could just be accepted as Anita and I, a place where I was accepted as Gordon.

On a rare afternoon free time when most of the other youngsters played pickup softball on the roughly laid out diamond, Anita and I walked down to the village of Palmer on Route 20. As the campground approached downtown, there was a high stone wall with a flat surface. I boosted Anita up to the top of the wall and she accepted my hand as she towered over me and walked beside me into town. At the tiny variety store I bought Anita a vanilla ice cream cone with chocolate "shots" which she ate with obvious gratitude and reaching over with her free hand took mine for the walk back to town.

Sunday evening came and the camp broke up. My parents arrived and again to their dismay I was reported as the one boy not saved in the course of the camp. No such expectation had been placed on Anita. If her parents cared, they never showed up to encourage her. Someone just picked her up and took her to Thomas Street Worcester. Before she left I made sure she wrote down her address in the little notebook we used for Bible Class.

Within a week, I dashed off a letter to Anita pouring out my heart and for the first time using the word love to describe my feelings to another human being. Each day I was awaiting the reply. The reply came in a quite unexpected way. As I scanned the following Wednesday's Worcester Telegram before beginning my deliveries, there it was among the obituaries. Anita Stoddard, 12 Thomas Street, age 11, hit by a motorist while riding her bicycle in downtown Worcester and died of her injuries on arrival at Hannlman Hospital. So ended first love.

CHAPTER 4
COMING OF AGE

end of innocence

Cousins, as I have said elsewhere, played an enormous role in shaping Junior, the only child of ageing working parents. Many cousins played their part but proximity to Margaret and Marion Brown, made these two, daughters of my mother's sister Annie, decisive in my first taste of real Sin. Annie, like my father, was a saved and sanctified Free Methodist.

But as next-door neighbors, sharing a common unpaved driveway, there was always tension between us. The drive led to our two car garage and the Browns never had a car and often depended on my father for a ride. Each winter the issue arose as to who would shovel the drive after snowstorms. For what had to be perverse reasons David Brown would shovel occasionally, but only his side. My father, in his sanctification would always forgive but it did rankle us. Now Margaret was the older of the sisters, a full six years older than me, and three years older than Marion. Margaret was unwaveringly Free Methodist, off to the church junior college of Roberts, just as I left elementary school. That left Marion, the emerging high-schooler living just across that controversial driveway.

It would have been as I entered the sixth grade that my mother entered Clinton Hospital for what I was later made aware was a hysterectomy. For the ten days she was in the hospital I was farmed out during the day to Aunt Annie, officially, but in fact to Marion, I, an 11-year-old in the care of a 14-year-old – but what a 14-year-old she soon turned out to be. Marion had exactly the same values and early church experiences as I had, but by 14, she was listening to other voices and indeed deep hormonal instincts and she was enthusiastically responding.

I was quickly brought into her confidence and willingly became a co-conspirator. And it was a conspiracy, already up and running. Of course we were forbidden to go to the movies and she was prohibited from exhibiting any makeup or jewelry. At that time, each of us had very modest access to money. My father left 25 cents on the windowsill for my allowance each morning. I had a regular morning paper route and a sometimes afternoon route from which I was lucky to clear four dollars a week. Most of that went to comic books: Superman, Batman, Submariner, and Wonder Woman! I kept up with them all. Marion had a steady babysitting job up on Water Street that brought her about five dollars a week. But Marion had a taste for the abundant life and was already well into it when she took charge of me at age eleven and brought me quickly to age and out of the Garden of Innocence.

For beginners it was easy deceptions. We could tell our parents that we never had enough of church. As they were anxious that the Free Methodists, few in numbers, had few programs for kids, Marion discovered the Baptist Christian Endeavor that met on Sunday afternoons, or so we would tell our parents. And I recall that on at least one or two occasions, we actually did go to the CE – and, of course, we were blissfully bored.

Marion had a more creative alternative. After Sunday lunch, she would come by and collect me and we would tell our parents that we were off again to church. On our way out to High Street, Marion would stop at a reflecting window and out came the lipstick and rouge and on went the faux-pearl necklace and the Woolworth birthstone ring. By the time we were on the main drag, the 14-year-old would have aged by three or four years. Everyone said she looked like the movie star, Deanna Durbin, but I had little base of comparison. So up High Street we would go, heading for the one o'clock matinee at the Strand, where the usher staff warmly greeted Marion and older guys would come sit on the other side of her. They would become readily friendly, which Marion obviously thought was just great but, at least for that first year, that was mostly it. At the end of the double feature we would reverse the procedure – back down High Street, off with the jewelry and makeup and a pleasant stock report to both sets of parents as to how much we enjoyed Christian Endeavor.

But as I entered seventh grade, the traffic became heavier. Looking back over the years through the eyes of my own teenagers, I can see now that both Marion and I were brighter and more mature than most kids and school became a bore. All four of our parents worked factory shifts beginning at seven in the morning and none got home before school ended at three fifteen. None of the four had themselves gone beyond the sixth grade of school so they had no measure by which to judge what we were supposed to learn in school.

The stage was set for a comprehensive plan of truancy. At first it was just staying home, mostly my emerging hormones driving me to finish my paper route, buy my stack of comic books and then return to Marion's house and climb – quite chastely, I hasten to add – right into her bed, she in her p.j.'s for most of the day, emerging in late afternoon to report to our parents as to what a great day we had in school. Without much effort or imagination we made this the pattern of our lives. Of course, there would be some expression of concern from our teachers.

Whether it was Marion's idea or mine, an inspiration occurred readily. After three consecutive days of skipping school altogether, on Friday the last day of school I would explain to my mother that I had suffered a severe headache during lunch on Friday. Miss Paine would want a note explaining my absence. "Here, mother, is what it should say. Dear Miss Paine, Gordon has been quite sick. Please excuse his absence. Lillian Graham." My mother would faithfully write the note and Miss Paine would in good faith receive and file it away confident that my mother was aware that my sickness had caused my extensive absence. Still, there were the report cards that carried a record of absences. "Simple," said Marion. "I have a copy of your mother's signature and I can produce the neatest forgery for you and nobody will be the wiser."

So on we went into forgery and a life of more serious crime. Since all four parents were loyal war workers they had fully cooperated with their employers' program of withholding weekly payments which went toward the purchase of War Bonds, usually in denominations which after ten years of maturity would yield $25, $50 or $100. From their experience of the Great Depression, neither set of parents trusted banks and they would happily store their bond certificates in metal boxes at the back of bureau drawers. Marion was the first to locate her parents' storehouse and I was enlisted to search out mine. Now, we were in the big time – federal offenses.

An almost casual routine. We would get on the school bus before eight and get off uptown in front of the post office. Into the Post Office Marion would confidently stroll. Up to the clerk and a presentation of a $50 war bond appropriately signed on the back for cashing. With a smile and a friendly wink, the bond was exchanged for $37.50 or whatever its short term maturity value was and off we would go across the street to the Worcester bus stop and we would be on the 8:15 bus to Central Massachusetts Sodom. At the bus station, we would have a cup of coffee and then into Barnard and Summers Department store where both she and I would be fitted with elegant, new outfits. We would change into them at the bus station and off we went to the Plymouth Cinema whose first double feature began at ten. We would be out by noon and then over to the Statler Hotel on Franklin Street for a turkey pie lunch finished just in time to make the one o'clock show at the Warner, another double feature, leaving in time to catch the three o'clock bus back to Clinton.

Occasionally, but not often, we would vary the routine and catch a Boston and Maine train into Boston's North Station, do our shopping on Washington Street and make a late afternoon trip back in time to report to our parents what a great day we had at school. Before boarding the homeward bound bus, Marion and I would go to the bus station lockers, take out again our school clothes, change back into them and drop our newly bought outfits in the trash.

In time, of course we became a familiar duo to older n'er-do-well guys on Worcester, street guys, mostly of Italian American background, reputedly gainfully employed along Shrewsbury Street in rackets of some sort or other. Birds of a feather do flock together and some of these wise guys saw Marion as a chick ready for plucking. But, it was largely just good fun. Two of the guys would come sit behind us in the Plymouth. One would lure me to sit with him a few rows back thus vacating my seat for his buddy. Buddy would explore Marion's developing anatomy while I was introduced a few rows back to the workings of a .45 automatic pistol, being shown how readily the clip could be removed and re inserted. I had no Freudian interpretation of the whole exercise at the time.

Like all good things, this little racket had to one day come to an end. There were early warning signs. My new 7th grade classmate, Sydney Schanberg, was clever from the beginning and would announce loudly almost within earshot of our teacher, "Miss Paine, Gordon would like to confess why he is skipping school." Obviously even the most obtuse of our classmates saw signs of our high living. After a time, Marion's mother indeed noticed the disappearance of war bonds from her storage place.

"No problem, mother," said Marion. "I will help you compose a letter to the FBI who will be interested in investigating." So, the letter was written to the Boston Office of the FBI. Marion then cheerfully offered that she and I would post it off in the afternoon mail. Torn up in pieces just as soon as we were out of sight, we were then obliged to fabricate a response. The next week we took the Boston train early into North Station. On the second floor of South Station there were batteries of Remington manuals for rent. Onto the top of the blank sheet Marion typed the letterhead: Federal Bureau of Investigation, Boston Office, etc. "Dear Mrs. Brown: Your letter of January 6, 1945 was received and noted. On the basis of the information you offered, we are unable to pursue the investigation further. But if we can be of any further help, do not hesitate to write us again. Respectfully, Martin J. Buchanan, Special Agent." Off it went with a Boston postmark making Aunt Annie just a little curious as to how J. Edgar Hoover got such a reputation as a crime-buster.

But a month or so later, my early life of crime came to an end. It was just greed and overreaching that caught up with me. Early one Tuesday morning, Marion called at my house "to see if Junior was ready to go to school." My mother was taking one of her rare sick days from work and heard the two of us go off. We were both on our regular 8:15 bus to Worcester although I remember having forebodings. But I got greedy.

Marion being instinctively shrewder figured this was not a day for two double bills. When we got out of the Plymouth at noon, she cautioned me, "your mother could well sense something was up, I'm taking the twelve o'clock bus home." "Just tell her that I won't be home for lunch," I said. "Tell her I am going to a noontime birthday party for Bobby Baer." At the time I sensed it wouldn't fly. Sure enough when my mother heard Marion's story, she gathered herself together and up to Corcoran School, she went to see Miss Paine. "Oh," said Miss Paine, "I am so glad you came up. I did mean to contact you. I have been worried about Gordon's attendance this year. You know he has missed 72 days already." Two wise women soon got the full picture.

I was on the three o'clock bus to Clinton and was about to get off at the Jenney Gas Station when I saw Donald and Malcolm McLeod waiting at the stop on their bikes. I stayed on to the next stop but they followed. Their message was simple, your mother knows. Resolute, I cockily entered my back door. My mother was lying on the living room couch. "My heart is broken," she said. "Your dinner is in the oven." "I don't care," I said arrogantly and went up to my bedroom and slammed the door.

Nothing more was said by my parents or Miss Paine when I went back to school the next day. But I was changed. From that January of the 7th grade until my high school graduation I never missed another day of school for whatever reason. When in my senior years Principal Eban Cobb suggested I take a day off to check out possible admission to Harvard, I agreed to do so only on the condition that he not mark me absent. Marion and I remained friends but her tremendous influence over me diminished in time. My innocence had been irrevocably lost, but in truth, I had few regrets. I was offered the fruit of the tree of knowledge of good and evil. It would have been a cop out to say that the woman gave it to me to eat. I did it all willingly and with pleasure not regretted to this day.

Years later, when in a Nazarene college, Marion claimed a born again experience and obliquely confessed to my parents with an extra ambivalent caveat, I love my cousin Junior and would never want to get him into trouble. And, I took her at her word and I loved her until she lost her mind and died a sad, lonely, guilt-ridden death.

Synagogue

landsman

yiddish: a fellow countryman

I never could quite figure out why from the very beginning I felt comfortable in the company of Jews – and they with me. It surely had something to do with my Free Methodism. The Clinton Jewish community experience closely paralleled that of the Free Methodists. Sometime after World War I, both communities expanded from their original core worshippers to the point where they were able to build their own house of worship. Up into the 1920s local Jews, built on an earlier generation of German Jews, mostly the Gould family, worshipped in Clinton's Town Hall. In turn the Free Methodists met for worship in the community room of the Daily Item newspaper. The synagogue was started on Water Street in 1925 and four years later following almost an identical building plan, the Free Methodist Church was built on my father's extra lot on High Street, almost across the street from a Gould homestead.

But for me personally, it was that post depression Jewish influx to Clinton from New York City that gave a face to Judaism. These were big-time Jews wise to the ways of the city, who came to Clinton, determined to do what it took to adjust and prosper. Most had the small businessman ethos – to which my father aspired without much to show for it – but, overall, the New York Jews came with what I would later know to call Yiddishakopf.

I was in the fourth grade when Al Cooperman, Donnie Jacobson, Anrie Fine, Mal Price, and Jerry Finkle first began to people my life. All were within two or three years of my age and all found themselves in the confounding milieu of a dominantly Irish Catholic public school system. We quickly bonded as fellow outsiders.

Jerry Finkle and Arnie Fine lived first in the three story tenement two doors down from me but clearly their family saw it as a transient arrangement and quickly built homes of their own. Donnie Jacobson lived for a time just down a block on High Street a few doors up from Alan and Selma Cooperman (children of Ben and Bertha, soon to become surrogate parents to me). Donnie's family moved on but Alan and his family connected with me then and remain connected now almost 55 years later.

Ben Cooperman was a man of many parts and had seen and been involved in the outside world. At one time, Ben had a promising career as a boxer. His family came from pre-revolution Russia when each Easter became a day of horror for those in the ghetto. He would recount how after the celebration of the Orthodox Easter, quite commonly, the local cadre of Cossacks would mount their horses and with bloody screams descend on gallop into the ghetto with swords flashing slashing out at Jews, adult and children alike, calling out "Christ Killers," bent on what they considered righteous vengeance. This story I heard long before the story of the then ongoing holocaust was known.

Ben and Bertie had reluctantly left Brooklyn where their larger family remained so that they could follow their runaway industry the Doll Factory that had fled radical unionization for the calmer pastures and grateful vacant mill owners of Clinton. Bertie was an accomplished office secretary and she remained working long enough to send Alan's sister Selma and Alan himself off for higher education. The work ethic and the learning of that ethic were foremost in the Cooperman family and I soon found it supportive of my fondest dreams.

Then there was the continuing New York City connection and the Jewish Music Hall and burlesque show raunchy humor. Alan soon shared with me the tribal secret that in their middle age crises, his parents and the Finkles went often to Boston's Old Howard strip shows to get some life going again in their respective marriages. When television finally arrived in the late forties, it was on the Cooperman's TV that I sat enjoying with them the New York Jewish humor of Milton Berle. These were my people.

But it got a bit too close at one time. I was told one week that Alan's close same-age cousin Phyllis would be up to Clinton for the weekend and that I was welcome to come meet her. I would have known her to be Alan's cousin on first sight. Here was an almost exact copy – albeit female – of the boy with whom I had shared the closest darkest secrets of our emerging sexuality. The transference was amazing. She immediately took to me and I didn't need words to communicate with her. She, Al and I watched the Milton Berle program together and just kept the set on as we sat comfortable in each other's presence. Alan, to his eternal credit, sensed what was going on, and announced himself tired and off to bed. Just as soon as he left the room, I got up and turned off the TV. Phyllis immediately melted into my arms as if we had courted for years. Nothing really was said and not much at any later time.

But immediately I knew that I had a serious identity crisis. Why kid myself? I was no Free Methodist. I was Jewish. These were my people – and if not Phyllis it would certainly be another Jewish girl sometime, someplace (as it turned out, there most surely

was). Ben and Bertha were incredibly understanding but pushed
me not a bit. The rabbi just came by one evening and they left the
room while the two of us talked. True to the Jewish non-
proselytizing custom, the rabbi gently tested my resolve.
Circumcision, happily, was already a fact, but what of my belonging
to a family and a different tradition. We agreed to put it on hold
for the moment – where effectively it has remained throughout
my life – freed up and put in healthy perspective by the Vatican II
doctrine of non-supercession, the understanding that Christians
have no interest in converting the once and forever Chosen People.
But for now I was off the hook with Phyllis. I visited her once
again in Coney Island and in our fifties we strolled the waterfront
in a small Massachusetts seaport. We still chat comfortably. She is
now divorced. She knows I am indissolvably married and we can
look back at a rare moment of happiness in our mid teens.

But Alan was not through with exposing me to the nicest of
Jewish girls, but to be on the safe side, no longer his cousins. We
devised a plot. He became acquainted with a quite lively set of
Jewish girls in Worcester. I would be palmed off as cousin Gordon
Schwartz of Brooklyn and under Alan's coaching, I would be
furnished with a sufficient vocabulary of trendy Yiddish phrases to
allow me to pass. And it worked well for our summer of 1949. But
with our dates around the table in Shrewsbury's Howard Johnson's
I blew my cover. We went around the table with our orders. When
it came to me I said impulsively: "Make mine fried clams." Gasps!
I looked around and picked up that I blown cover. To add to my
stupidity, I offered, "Well, what the heck. It is Friday." To this day
in some circles of the Clinton and Worcester communities, I am
heckled regularly and called: "Schwartzy." You know what? That
makes me sort of proud.

uptown to school

As the 1942 school year ended at Parkhurst, we knew we would be breaking up as a class. Those on the west side of Counterpane Brook would be off to the two-room Major Walsh School on Main Street and some would move into the huge Corcoran Elementary School, which had all of seven grades and ten classrooms. The remainder, among which I found myself, would be relegated to the two-classroom "Chicken Coop," whose formal name was the Major McRell. Clinton seemed to have spawned more than its share of majors in the World War I Expeditionary Forces but with the intensive school building of the 1920s, each had a namesake school.

Corcoran School

Moving uptown meant mingling for the first time with the Cedar Hill elite. Most had been in school together from first grade in Corcoran with a new element coming from the fifth grade at Water Street's Bowers (Charles Bowers, atypically, had been a prominent protestant pastor, and no major) Elementary School. But, to me as a north-ender I felt much the outsider. There was a clique consisting of the Mortons, Jaquiths, Prestons, and Schanbergs, who seemed to have known each other forever and whose parents were shop owners and lawyers and in touch with what went on Uptown.

But it was broad and stolid Miss Broderick who made me most welcome in her chicken coop – she the mother hen. We could hear the strident younger Miss Tierney chastising her seventh grade charges next door. But life in the sixth grade – before I had fallen into my truancy stage – was spent adjusting and enjoying. My favorite pastime was catching the always-present houseflies on my desk top, dipping them into the ink well, clipping off their wings, and watching them trek ink marks across the desk top. It was that year also that I perfected my comic skill of folding up my ears into my head and playing all I could for laughs with my new classmates. The one academic accomplishment of that year which I retain duly documented in my childhood King James Bible is an essay written in April of 1945, on the occasion of V-E Day, when in my youthful informed prescience I distinguished between the Western Allies and their Soviet Union colleagues to the East. I would have had throughout that year both a morning and afternoon paper route that kept me in pocket money and made me precociously wise to the ways of the world. From the Chicken Coop I was duly promoted to Miss Paine's Corcoran School Seventh Grade and that year is most accurately reported in my chapter on the end of innocence.

corning

The eighth grade in Corning School was an introduction to secondary education. No more morning and afternoon sessions: now four periods running from eight to one. My homeroom was with Margaret O'Toole who taught English Grammar. As we rotated classes clockwise I would then go to Miss Burke for introductory algebra, up to the indomitable Mary Davis for English literature and then to young vibrant Sarah McNally for American History. I really engaged with all four of them. My one residual bit of mischief was to arrive at school just before the 8:10 tardy bell, thus missing the daily salute to the flag and prayers. The School built on the standard four-room brick model was particularly ugly, set in a rock-scrabble yard, ironically at the corner of Grove and Pleasant Streets. The significant social initiative of the year was suiting up all us boys in cast off high school basketball uniforms and sending us across Chestnut Street, to the State Guard Armory where we played teams of the other eighth grades, from St.John's and Holy Rosary Catholic School. It was there that I first encountered Jim Arsenault, Jim McNally and Brennie Bailey whose lives were to later intertwine with mine in high school.

That was the year when teachers sorted out who was teachable and who disposable, and to my great surprise I was identified with the former. I knew for sure one day as I had a routine fight during recess with the school scrapper, Alan "Bimbo" Chase. As Bimbo and I scrambled in the dirt not quite able to get the best of each other, I felt a strong hand on the back of my neck, as I was hoisted out of the dirt by my homeroom teacher Margaret O'Toole. Into her room I was marched. "Gordon", she said. "You can spend the rest of your days scrambling in the dirt with Alan Chase, or with

your brains, you can make something of yourself!" Just what I
needed to hear and it was twenty years to pass when at her brother's
funeral I was able to take her aside and tell her with choked voice
how important that little lecture had been to my future.

Corning school

From the perspective of a roundly educated adulthood, I can
now look back on those eighth grade courses as the basic building
blocks of what was to come. Eighth grade then, of course, would
be junior high today – the beginning of the coherent, hourly course
instruction, which I was fated to follow into college, law school
and finally theological seminary. It was there I learned the four
basic educational building blocks: language, literature, mathematics
and history.

Margaret O'Toole's diagrams of sentences can still be pictured
in my mind. Every word we speak or write must relate to another,
be connected in relationship and become the mechanisms of logical
thought. I was made ready for Latin and then French. Gaps, as

well as sequences, set off reactions in my thought processes. I was hooked on language skills – although you might not be able to tell it from this recounting.

And so, it was with Miss Burke's Algebra. Our first encounter with relationship came with the mysterious X's and Y's. How indeed could we establish relationships so that with only one known quantity, we could derive a value for the remaining unknowns? My only regret, looking back now, was that we were not early or even simultaneously required to use this process in the real world of physical and biological science. A gap in my education, which I feel even today.

Mary Davis' love affair with literature, especially the American poets, was borne out in her long career and we shared only what was left, but it was still substantial. Being challenged to recite by memory 25,000 lines of poetry was my most pleasant task that year. The first stanza of Longfellow's "Evangeline" still resonates in my memory:

> "This is the forest primeval
> The murmuring pines and the hemlocks
> Beaded with moss indistinct in the twilight ..."

Were the echoes there from the folk memories of my classmates – children of emigrants uprooted by circumstance and sent to live in a strange new place?

Sarah McNally, someday to marry the legendary Bingo McMahon, was still a sprightly, confident, attractive young woman charged with drilling American History dates into our most hesitant heads. What did it all mean? How can I look back on it as a product of Harvard's great history department of the 1950s? Well, again it was a foundation – but how narrow and parochial were teachers in those days on the saga of history. And of course, it all began in 1492 with the arrival of the White Man on these shores. But in those days, that was the way Harvard taught it as well.

Somehow, I never learned, in over eight years of required college courses for my major that there were people here on these shores when the Europeans arrived. The American Southwest was Spanish in its settling and we Anglophones took over largely by deceit and force of arms. However, such deconstruction would have to wait for the passing of two more decades and even today, I have to ask myself, in my new Irish citizenship, whose history indeed is being taught? But, for her time and her preparation, it was Sally McNally who first implanted the seed which grew to make me a history major.

trixie

I still need to be guarded in telling the story of Trixie. I will be changing names of all concerned – other than, of course, my own. Not to protect the innocent. None of us involved was innocent – certainly not Trixie at 14. Trixie had already been "putting out" for a year – mostly for older guys, but we 16-year-olds hung about hoping somehow that Trixie would share what she had with one or the other of us.

The hanging out was easy. Trixie's father ran a floral business out of a downtown location. Trixie covered the office for her father who made his delivery runs – after school and often into the evening. When he dropped by to collect orders he would see us and give us a fishy look. He surely had a good idea what was going on. Otherwise, why would he have thrown "Clapper".McGrail over the banister of his home when he just found Clapper and Trixie talking?

And we let Trixie know that we knew, not in the most subtle of ways. We would sit there and blow up condoms as she giggled and asked why we bought the junior size. Bright, alert, composed— that was Trixie at 14.

And literary as well. That was the year I took a study period in Clip McNamara's English I Class. I sat in the back – just behind Trixie. I assume she provided quite conventional book reports for Clip but she went on a quite different compositional tangent for me. We sort of knew at the time that if there was anything around to be got, our starting fullback, Zip Billings would be getting it. Zip had an advantage. Zip's father was the protestant undertaker and between funerals and on Sundays Zip had use of the Cadillac limousine. On a lucky Sunday afternoon, Zip could make two and even three runs out to make-out heaven – poorly patrolled Willow Road. An easy-going, if totally qualmless guy, Zip had no idea that he might become a literary figure.

But Trixie had him down in writing. She would pass back the page torn from her lined notebook and I would be asked to correct her spelling and grammar. Hardly a misspelled word and it read like a ballad. Zip's every move was down there more neatly than any T formation play from Bingo's playbook. Zip would stop the car in a grove of trees. He would suggest that Trixie take off just her lower garments and climb into the back seat. Zip would then carefully divest himself of all his garments: jacket, shirt, tie, trousers, shoes and socks and fold everything neatly on the front seat. He would then jump into the back seat astride the pantyless Trixie. Then the lyrics of Trixie's ballad would begin, courtesy of her reading of Shakespeare's "Anthony and Cleopatra." Trixie became Cleopatra. She stroked and cuddled Zip's "asp" watching it rise and writhe amidst his appreciative moaning. And then, only then did she allow the asp to find its hole and with mutual and deliberative movements it concluded and Zip was out and up and carefully dressing and combing his hair to return to his appointed rounds. I was at a loss as to what to say to Trixie for her confidence in my critical judgment but I suspect she found what she was really looking for when she noticed the prominent bulge in the front of my trousers.

But that was as far as it ever went with Trixie and me. Only once did I dare to ask her for date and that was to the quite public carnival in Ash Street Playgrounds. There we sat stationary for ten minutes on the top of the Ferris wheel. She looked at me fondly. I made stuttering small talk. But she was content to let it go at that, good friends, but she knew I was fated to live out my high school days a very horny and literate virgin.

junior airman

From those early years of Sunday afternoon walks, Bolton Airport represented freedom. Under Free Methodist ethos, the only allowable Sunday afternoon activities were walks. They, for my mother and me, and later for me and Cousin Marion, were either up to the family lot at Woodlawn Cemetery, or off over the hills and through the hardwood forest of Woodward Heights to Bolton Airport. Piper Cubs, Cessna, high-winged and low-winged monoplanes and even an occasional biplane spelt travel and adventure. For two dollars you could sit in the closed cabin of a Piper Cub or, better still, in the front cockpit of a biplane and after a rough and bumpy taxi across the cow pasture field, you were up in the air to see Clinton, the Wachusetts Reservoir, and all the wide, wide world. My mother first treated me to a flight on my tenth birthday and I was hooked. At least twice a month, on my paper route earnings, I was off, often by myself, for yet another up, up and away over the wide, wide world of Central Massachusetts.

I must have been about fourteen when I first heard about the Civil Air Patrol chapter starting up at Bolton Airport. The rough and ready boys from the North End, the Miltons, the Floyds, and Mitch McInermy would have been the ones to first hear about it. Already they had tinkered with cars and being an airplane mechanic was the ultimate of their ambitions. And however different I was made to feel from them, with our books and strict lifestyle, at fourteen I shared their dreams and on Tuesday evenings, I hiked the three miles to Bolton and sat in the cold hangar while the struts and canvas which composed Piper Cubs were gone over with us and we were urged to write it all down because there would be a test later. But, for me, interest sagged and I never remember taking the test.

But then, in the winter of 1949, before my 16th birthday, the official letter arrived from the United States Air Force Reserves in Boston. My name had been suggested as a possible recruit for a soon-to-be-formed Fighter Interceptor Reserve Wing to be headquartered at Otis Air Base on Cape Cod, adjacent to the old Camp Edwards where World War II troops had been marshaled before embarking to the European theatre. Wow, World War II was still a warm and exciting memory for me. My parents' foster children, Eddie and Jesse Samples had sent me powerfully descriptive stories of combat in the South Pacific. Sands of Iwo Jima had recently played to full houses in the Strand cinema. The American military had just been reorganized under President Truman in anticipation of a prolonged Cold War. The old Army Air Corps had now been transformed into a new service on equal footing, a US Air Force, and I was being recruited to be one of its first members. Paul Floyd called and asked if I was interested. I sure am, I told him. "They are forming in February," said Paul. "Should we hitchhike to the Cape and check it out?" "Sure thing," I replied.

Then the yellow flag went up. A second letter came. This one from the Attorney General of the Commonwealth of Massachusetts. "You may have been the recipient of a letter," it said, "but if you are not yet 18 or 17 with parents' permission, it does not apply to you." A quick check with Paul, better known as "Gabby". "Who's to know?" said Gabby. "We could easily pass for 18," he suggested. "We have done it before." "I'm game," I replied. And off we went to the Cape, Friday afternoon after school, the second Friday of February, 1950. I have no memory of what we told our parents. Surely nothing about that second letter. So off we went.

Otis was set in the sand and scrub oak of the Lower Cape, outside Falmouth. We had been to Hyannis Beach and we knew that there was a nearby rotary where one of the roads spoking off led to Otis Air Base. We arrived in the Reception Area, a quadrangle of old two story wooden barracks with an Orderly Room on the roadside. Lots of guys and two women were sitting on the steps of the barracks. None was under 25 and all were World War II veterans of the Army Air Corps, the women, in the auxiliary, WACs. Somehow, Gabby and I just blended in. Off we went with the guys to the Enlisted Men's Club where our still virginal palates were introduced to Millers' High Life, "the champagne of bottled beer," and for only ten cents a bottle. The next morning we lined up and were issued clothing, still the khaki and olive drab of World War II, but with the directions that we were to begin dyeing our boots black because the new US Air Force would soon be fitted with spiffy dark blue uniforms and our boots would need to match.

Gabby and I were then lined up with others to take our oath of office into the Air Force. Two-by-two we entered the chaplain's office. Fitted in our uniforms, Gabby and I were nervous as we stood together in front of the chaplain's desk. He was solemn. "Raise your right hands", he directed, "and repeat after me". "I – then your first second and last names – do solemnly swear". Paul and I raised our hand, he first his left, but noticing me, he dropped the left and raised his right. "I," I began, "George Gordon Graham" . . . Paul began: "I, George Gordon . . . I, George Gordon Floyd, do solemnly swear …" The chaplain did not notice, but I started to break down and giggle. Paul continued straight-faced, but I could hardly get the rest of the words out. As we finished, the chaplain could not let my giggling go unacknowledged. "Gentlemen," he intoned, "you have just been sworn into the service of the United States Air Force. This is a solemn occasion, no laughing matter". While I am sure my face was still a dark shade of red, I did compose myself enough to offer a few "yes sirs" and off we were into our new career.

By March and April meetings, Paul and I had settled into a good routine, having hooked up with a sergeant from Worcester who picked us up at home and drove us up and back to the Cape with a couple of other guys, also sergeants who had spent years in England or the South Pacific and regularly swapped war stories and sang long choruses of Lilly from Piccadilly. In March I observed my 16th birthday but made no mention of it to my new buddies.

By April, Paul and I were granted tentative MOSs (Military Occupational Specialties),both jet plane mechanics. Each Saturday and Sunday morning, a 2 1/2 ton truck would arrive at the barracks and he and I and a couple of other guys would jump on and off we would go to a shack in the middle of the airfield where there was a pot of coffee and lots of comic books and there we would sit until the truck arrived to take us back later in the day. We had little or no contact with the pilots. As in most air services, they were college graduates, commissioned officers and all we observed was their arrival and departure from their brand new jet fighters, of which we had ten, as they drove in and out of the control center in staff cars. But rumors reached us. The most ominous was the one of the court martial of a second lieutenant. Against standing regulations, he had chosen on a dare to dive his new jet from high altitudes down almost to sea level and in so doing had unofficially broken the sound barrier. Not only that, but his plane suffered severe damages. We could see it parked there now permanently, ripples of the aluminum up and down the fuselage. The ruling of the Court Martial, we were told , required a dunning of his pay for a period of four years until the $120,000 worth of damages he had caused were repaid. Soon thereafter, our sergeant asked for volunteers to go out on the runway and guide a jet fighter in for a landing with a set of flags. Whatever daring I had previously aspired to as a jet mechanic was ruined by the news of that court ruling and I never did get to do anything other than read comic books during my months as a jet mechanic.

June was coming up and this was the occasion for us "weekend warriors" to do a more extensive two week training tour at Otis. I was then a high school junior and the more promising scholars and athletes were chosen that month to attend Massachusetts Boys State, a mock state government body, set up by the local American Legion posts at the University of Massachusetts. Both my football and debating team coaches indicated that they would very much

like to nominate me as part of the six-boy delegation. Alas, I had
to tell them, I was off to the Cape to do my military service.
Somehow nothing about this response from a 16-year-old seemed
to trouble them. So off went Gabby and myself, the second week
in June 1950, excused from the last two weeks of school.

The week of training went smoothly. Each day was crammed
with courses on military codes of conduct, on safe sex, on chains of
command and all the basics that made an informed soldier. And
each night there were our Millers High Life beer in the EM Club,
as we listened to the then current tunes of "On Top of Old Smokey"
and "Blueberry Hill." Gabby and I were just two of the guys.

I can't really remember what Gabby did that intervening
weekend, but I hitchhiked the 100 miles back to Clinton on
Saturday afternoon and on schedule left after lunch on Sunday for
the return on Route 128 to the Cape. I reached 128 about three
o'clock and the driver who picked me up had the car radio on.
"Did you hear the news?" he asked, as I hauled my duffle bag on
board. "What news?" I asked. "Well," he said, "seems like North
Korea has attacked South Korea and President Truman has called a
special session of the United Nations Security Council and it appears
we will soon be at war . . . General MacArthur has been ordered
from Japan to lead a United Nations force into South Korea to
slow down the North Korean offensive." "Wow", I said and sat
back in my seat wondering what would come next.

When I was delivered to the Otis Airbase gate, for the first
time during my brief service the gate was guarded by two armed
MPs who checked my ID card. As I walked to the barracks I noticed
that the huge radar antennae were spinning on their base. In the
barracks there was panic. My more senior WW veterans were
gathered in a group. The weekend larks of "dime beers" and chance
to get away from the "old lady" were now history. Telegrams were
being composed and sent to congressmen, pointing out their heavy
family duties, real and imagined physical and psychological
handicaps. The mood was unanimous. We want out.

More reality sank in on Monday morning. We were called to an assembly of all units, reserve and active, in the base cinema. There on the stage, with the screen rolled up, were four of our commissioned officers, now dressed as Soviet Officers, uniforms somehow having been provided. A mock drill was put on in dead seriousness. "We are the Soviet Air Force General Staff," we were told. "This is 25 June 1950 and we are planning a bombing mission to take out New York City, which will paralyze telecommunications for all the Eastern United States. We will send two planes with nuclear bombs, over the North Pole, which will evade American radar. We will drop the two bombs and ditch the planes off the New Jersey coast, where a submarine waiting off the coast will pick up the crews. The only impediment to our plan," said the "Soviet Officers," "is the 50th Fighter Interceptor Reserve Wing now on Cape Cod. They alone stand between us and the successful mission on New York City." I could feel the collective shudder go through the bodies of the 500 men and women there assembled.

So I felt no particular cowardice when I asked to see the commanding colonel at ten the next morning. He was seated looking very much a colonel. "Colonel," I began, "I have a confession to make. You see, all along I have been lying about my age." The color rose from the colonel's neck right up onto his receding hairline. "Do you realize, young man what can now happen to you? You can be court-martialed for swearing a false oath and made to pay back all money you received, including your meals, and other benefits. What I am going to do for you, as a favor, is to ask you not to tell anyone else. You just collect all your uniforms and equipment and turn it over to your first sergeant and get the hell off this base before I change my mind!! Do you hear me!" Sure, I heard him and I was out of his office in a flash. Off to the barracks I ran, off with the khakis, on with the civvies. Jam everything into my duffle bag and present it to the sergeant. "Here you are sergeant," I said, summoning up my best military bearing. "This is for you. Just talk to the colonel, he will explain." And off I went to the gates, not looking back. Out to Route 128, back to Clinton and the normal life of a senior at Clinton High, a bit the wiser and considerably older from the experience.

And a postscript to the story. The strange brown envelope arrived the summer of 1954 when I was home for the summer from college. It was US Department of Defense envelope and there within was a lovely frameable certificate signed by the Secretary of the Air Force, acknowledging four years of honorable service of George Gordon Graham in the Air Force (Reserves) of the United States of America. When, the following August I was conscripted into the US Army in those days of the universal draft, there I was the one and only draftee in the US Army already collecting pay for four years longevity. But that's another story.

As an entirely unanticipated boon from my short air force career, I became, for a time, quite officially of age before my time. Having entered into the initial deception of moving my birth date back from 1934 to 1932 to meet the entrance requirements at my actual age of 15, I found myself leaving all my military baggage behind me on my day of truth in June 1950 with the singular exception that I still had in my wallet an official Air Force ID card saying I was then 18. Cards in those days were a simple piece of cardboard and easily altered. Just a little scratch-out of the "2" from the "32", replace it with a "0" and presto! I was, at true age 16, documented as 20 and the following March, my last year in high school, there I was "officially" 21, fully of age.

This of course made me eligible to drink alcohol. The prior New Year's Eve, my surrogate mother, Bertie Cooperman encouraged son Alan and me to toast in the New Year with a tiny glass of cherry herring, a soothing Vick's cough medicine mixture. The effect was warming and congenial and I had found the right place for alcohol at that time in my life – age 16. But then in that last year of high school, the peer pressure to drink until drunk took over. At the Polish American Club, it was easy. "Are you sure you're 21?" they would ask. "Pravda," I would confidently assert, proud of my command of Polish. And the Polish girls loved it. My friend Henry would accompany me there for a few brews on Saturday evening, fresh from Confession with Father Bascardi. With a couple of beers under his belt, his libido would again escape. As the nubile women took to the floor to polka with each other, Henry would look remorsefully into his dime beer. "No use, Gordo," he would lament. "I've had a near occasion of sin and can't receive tomorrow." Thus, I was introduced to alcohol and sin and the strange pre-Vatican II notion of the Eucharist. I'm sort of glad that it was Jewish Bertie Cooperman who gave me a more cheering introduction to the Devil's Brew.

homesick

Twice in my youth I panicked when away from home and significantly I sought out my cousin Marion as intermediary to ask my mother to arrange my coming home.

The first occasion was when I attended Cub Scout Camp in the summer of 1943. Earlier that year, high school math teacher Raymond Dyer and his Boy Scout son, Ray Jr., began for the first time a Cub Scout program for us nine-year-olds. As it was wartime, the appeal was mainly the blue uniforms with caps and kerchiefs. We reported weekly to the VFW Hall and were drilled in posture and marching and how to tie knots, all the skills which Baden Powell thought character building for English Schoolboys. So when spring turned to summer and the exciting prospect of camping in the New Hampshire woods was put before us, I enthusiastically signed up for the first two-week session at Camp Winocksett, at the foot of majestic Mt. Monadnock.

Cub scouting was an innovation at Winocksett and the first problem arising was where to put us young'uns. I recall there were only four or five of us pioneers among about 150 older scout campers. On a high rise above the camp playing and drilling fields there was a string of five staff cabins where 17-and 18-year-old cooks and bottle washers lived. We were moved in with them – and it was not a comfortable fix. We were out of the main life of the camp. Our most dramatic involvement was that we – but not our staff cabin mates – were expected to respond to the seven o'clock revelry and run down the steep grass slope in our altogether and skinny dip with all the scouts in the freezing mountain lake. Although in later life I quite liked cold swims, this at that time became a frightening and unavoidable exercise in torture. Thus, being initially put off by our separation from communal life I found this exercise in forced togetherness totally unpleasant. That, coupled with one dreadful gastronomical ordeal – wherein having mistakenly poured salt instead of sugar on my porridge, I was forced to sit there and eat the whole revolting bowlful. By that first Thursday, I scraped together a handful of coins, took myself to the camp's one pay telephone, called Cousin Marion and begged her to tell my parents that I wanted to come home. On Friday my father came and collected me, just slightly scarred by having wimped out of my first camping experience.

The second experience of homesickness took place three years later, when for reasons that now make no sense to me, I approached my parents with a firm desire to go to boarding school for my high school education. Not the traditional New England boarding schools, mind you, not having any acquaintance with their existence, but rather the high school prep program run by our one known Free Methodist college, Roberts Junior College, just outside Rochester, New York. I suppose at the time, my next-door cousin Margaret had graduated from their secretarial program, but it was for me a shot in the dark. Looking back, of course, it was at that stage of my life when I was returning to disciplined behavior: having been caught in my delinquency in the seventh grade, I had applied myself diligently to my eighth grade studies, without so much as a day of absence. My childhood smoking habit had been put on hold so that, although there was certainly no religious tug toward piety I suspect I viewed a Free Methodist School as the control over my life which I could never willingly surrender to my parents. So the last Friday in August of 1947, my mother and I, with my parents' huge Cunard Line steamer trunk full of a year's outfits, boarded a coach at the Worcester New York Central Depot bound for an overnight journey to Rochester. In Rochester, a taxi sent from the school met us, and by midmorning, I was duly enrolled as a high school freshman and my mother was on the afternoon train back to Worcester.

Again, it was an issue of housing and roommates. Since the high school component of the college was largely composed of locals – Roman Catholics indeed – I was assigned to a huge room with five double-decker bunks, a 13-year-old left with mainly 18- and 19-year-olds. In some ways I was up to it and joined in the excitement of it all. Whatever the home lifestyle of my roommates, they quickly evolved into typical college freshmen hellions. The second day there we salvaged a classic pair of trap-door men's long underwear and duly attached a paper sign that read "The Dean" and toward midnight sneaked out of our dorm and hoisted it up the flag pole. Great high spirits, but soon I knew I was out of my league. I was the only guy among the ten of us who seemed to ever need sleep. I never recovered from the overnight train ride. Even before formal classes the following Wednesday I was again on the phone with Cousin Marion. "Please, please, have my parents telegraph enough money for a train ticket home," I begged. The money came by Western Union within the hour and I was on the train the next day, soon back at Clinton High, but in the coming months, I paid a high price, academically and socially, for my late start there.

I suppose it can be said in both instances that I suffered not so much as a sickness for home – but was rather testing out those alternative environments into which I could fit and adjust. For it was barely two years later when I was happily spending weekends in military barracks at Otis Airbase with a bunch of World War II veterans as bunkmates – of course that's another story dealt with elsewhere.

wheels

Our generation can be said to have come to age with the American Dream of mass produced and available family autos. Elsewhere I have related my mother and my visit to the 1938 Flushing Meadow's World Fair and our ride in a futuristic GM car over the highway built on stilts. Then, of course, came the War and the conversion of Detroit to war production. But I grew up with an auto museum in my back yard. There, between us and High Street, north of the church, was an automobile graveyard full of just about every make of car turned out by Detroit between 1930 and 1940. Meleen's Garage, I suspect, got them to scavenge for spare parts, but as soon as Meleen closed (and on Saturdays, as Seventh Day Adventists they were regularly closed) we boys just opened the doors, got behind the wheel, opened the rumble seats for the youngest and with noisy muffler sounds, worked the gears and in fantasy took to the major highways that ran past Meleen's front door.

My family – unlike others – seemed always to have had a car. Never a new one but usually a 2-or 3-year-old bought from Meleen's who were hesitant to pass on a clinker to a next-door neighbor. For a year or two, when my father was full time with Furst McNess Home Products, we had two vehicles: the 1938 Chevy that would last us through the War as well as the neat little panel truck with the F-McNess logo. But that didn't last. Once again my father went broke in his desperate efforts to be an independent businessman and indeed to pay off the debit with the company he was forced to sell the Chevy and go through the humiliation of actually begging my mother for the loan of money so he could once again buy a car – then a postwar 1948 Ford V-8, which was to become the centerpiece of my high school social life. But to acquire regular access to that car I had to await my father's disabling heart attack – just after my 16th birthday.

As boys at Clinton High, we yearned for a car. I took more care to get a near-perfect grade in John "Piggy" Burke's drivers ed than I did in any academic subject. As the Tau Sigma Dinner Dance and Prom approached, getting one's license became critical. My father was hardly aware of the practice I had unofficially logged on that V-8. One of the few incentives I had to accompany him to his round of camp meetings was to await the visitation of the spirit on him at the Campgrounds when he would forget to hide his car keys and I would be off on the camp paths and onto the highways – back in the days of few highway patrols.

I reached my 16th birthday in March of my junior year. I quickly enlisted an older friend and good sport Billy DeCesari, whom I knew not at all well to go with me to the Worcester Registry Office to take the verbal exam which one needed to pass before the road test. Billy and I sauntered up to the examiner's window with a strategy in mind. The tough questions would be on distances: how near a fireplug could you park; how many feet before you can stop a car driving 40 mph, and such. However high a grade I may have achieved in Piggy's class, that Tuesday afternoon in Worcester it was all a blur. I needed that license by Friday to be able to take my own car for the Tau Sigma dance at the Meadows. So I would count on Billy's cues. I was sure to know at least whether the answer would be in feet or yards, whether in the tens or the hundreds. The rest I could count on Billy to feed me. So on with the question, "How far behind a fire apparatus may one safely follow as it is on its way to a fire?" Sure, I thought, it was in the hundreds of feet. And yep, Billy was literally on his toes as he began to tap out the answer. "One, two," I heard. The answer came out instinctively: "Two hundred feet," I said confidently. Then I heard the three more taps – too late. "Wrong," the man said. "You failed, but you can come back next week and try again. Damn! I would have to double-date with Alan and sit in the back seat for our ride to Framingham's Meadows. The next week I passed, of course, but too late to even get a decent date for the prom and my social life was on hold.

But not for long. Late that summer came my father's heart attack and the car was mine. The hitch of course was that I would have to do the circuit of his long time customers and give them the sob story about the finality of my father's disability and entreat them, in each instance, to purchase a year or more supply of their favorite product. More delicately, I was given the awkward task of collecting on years and years of overgenerously offered credit that gave me immediate insight into my father's regular failures in business. But I was also now learning of those humble people – most from Protestant Ulster – upon whom my father's limited business and social life depended.

Some of the women I visited had clearly in the past had some romantic interest in my father. Now widowed or never married, they were accustomed to welcoming my father, as they now did me, to sit at their kitchen table and chat each other up encouragingly – until, at the moment of departure, they felt often obliged to buy that bottle of vanilla flavoring or menthol rub for chest colds, just to make the visit worth George's time. These women were warm and sympathetic and they readily paid up their debits and took extra stock off my hands for cash.

Then there were the bachelor Wales brothers, who lived with their mother until her death, and who worked a hard lifetime in the wire mills. Their favorite remedy was the Furst McNess Vitamin B tonic, which came in pint bottles selling at two dollars each. The recommended daily dose was three heaping teaspoons before each meal to whet the appetite. It is important to note that as strict Baptists, Alex and Bobby looked proudly back on a lifetime of total abstinence. But a little light went on in my head when Alex in response to my entreaty to help sell out my father's stock decided to order ten cases of this tonic with each case being made up of twelve pint bottles. A good long term, perhaps lifetime supply, I thought for a couple of old codgers already in their sixties. The mystery cleared when I read the small print of the contents of each bottle. Comprised of yeast, wheat and barley, it also said clearly "12% alcohol." Thus cleared up the tonic habits of my father's tea-totaling friends.

But life with that Ford was not all work. That was the spring of the sensational pitching duo of Clinton High and summer American Legion baseball. Angie Bazyldo and Billy Stuka, now it would seem incredible, had between them pitched four no-hitter games in one year, with Stuka even pitching one perfect game where no one even reached base. The usually football-mad town turned baseball mad. And away games were moving further and further West as the teams moved up the ladder to state championships. So there were spring afternoons when the medicines were tossed back into the cellar. I brought the car to school empty and when the release bell rang at one, every attractive girl fan in the school knew what a soft touch Gordie was for a ride out to Northampton.

As my family obligations lessened and I gained confidence in the car, there now were Friday nights for the boys – off to the fleshpots of Webster's State Line Casino or even down to Boston's striptease emporium – the Old Howard with Rose La Rose and wonderfully raunchy Jewish comedians. Neither place regularly checked ID's and even when they did, I was certifiably already 21 or so it said on my Air Force ID card. Those rides down to Boston were daredevilish, as I often let all cylinders do their thing in excess of 100 mph going down the last stretch of Route 2 as we neared Boston.

But the nearest to a fatal crash I experienced in those days was on the way home from a well-disguised trip by Syd Schanberg. Mitch McInerney and me on a Saturday night to the State Line. My cover was plausible. Syd and I were then first string debaters on Bob Murphy's team. My partner was Caroline Keiger and his Mary Patrinos and that was well known to both sets of parents. So it seemed quite natural that in a year of banquets and balls we should need a car so that he and I could pick up dates and go to the National Forensic banquet. But of course we have something quite different in mind: a night of rum cokes and strippers at the State Line.

Syd and I had come to know and like McInerney from quite different angles. Mitch had been a mate in that Air Force Reserve romp at Otis Air Base and had gone on to star in basketball. Syd, in broadening his college application had served as manager of the basketball team. Mitch was no scholar and light relief for both of us. So it promised to be a good night out. And so it was when we cut out just before midnight for the 20 miles back to Clinton. We had each had about three drinks and all three of us sat up front, dozing off from time to time as we drove homeward.

All went well until we approached the Clinton line on a long straightaway of Route 110. Again I was tempted to see what those eight cylinders would do on a straight stretch. Down to the floor went the accelerator: sixty, seventy, eighty, coming up toward 100 when I hit the stretch of sand. We began to spin around. Mitch was jolted awake and started a fast version of the rosary. This woke up Syd, who, sensing the spin around of the car from the changing patterns before the windshield, began screaming. But as has been so common in my life of periodic crises, the adrenalin just rushed to my head and by the time the Ford hit the pine tree with its rear end I had revised the story I was to tell my father.

"Actually, we did also take in a movie Dad, and when we had come out we found that someone with a load of wood had backed into your car," I lied. He was skeptical but had no choice but to take my word for it. Soon thereafter to the surprise of his customers and to my personal chagrin he recovered almost fully from his coronary, went back to supplying Vitamin B to his tea-totaling cronies and recouped exclusive use of our family "wheels." But having thus blazed upon the big-time social scene, I was prepared to be content with the assurance that I would soon be off to college.

CHAPTER 5
ON THE OUTSIDE

my outsider year

Having entered Clinton High two full weeks later than my class-mates, I had some catching up to do, educationally and socially. I was given little choice of courses: Latin from the soon to be leg-endary coach Bill "Bingo" McMahon; Algebra from Ray Dyer; General Science from John Gibbons and English from John "Clip" McNamara. I fell far behind for the entire semester in Algebra and Latin, grades that would haunt me in my efforts to eventually graduate with honors. However, "Clip's" English class was a joy from the start. I had never had a teacher so determinably ironic or when challenged, just downright sarcastic. He taught me how to read classics such as Dickens and to turn in a thoughtful book review every Friday and it was returned to you on Monday all marked up by someone who cared to read you and challenge your grammar and style. Clip had a limited following, but I was a stead-fast fan right up through his old age when he suffered in some bitterness.

This was also the year of "released time" education. Each Monday at twelve we were released from school to go to our own church or synagogue and get religious instruction. It was only recently I learned that a classmate, whose father was a distinguished attorney, anticipated this clear violation of the First Amendment and made his daughter undergo the embarrassment of remaining in school. But initially, I just went with the system, going each Monday, with my only companion, Barbara Karras to the Free Methodist parsonage next to my home. Reverend Parker would start the hour session reading the first chapter of Genesis and then read Clark's Commentary on that passage; Barbara would be asked to read the second and then Parker would read the Commentary;

and then my turn with the third and round and round we'd go
until the hour mercifully would be up. I wanted out and my
memory was that Barbara got out first using some pretense or
other, leaving me alone with Rev. P. So my creative mind was brought
to bear. "Reverend Parker," I ventured one Monday. "The high
school doesn't think this works with me as your only pupil. They
have suggested I better stay in school." Of course, I had made this
up. I never told Joe McCaffrey, my homeroom teacher. So off I
would shoot each Monday at noon. But the parsonage was not my
destination. I would follow High Street just down as far as Maury's
Poolroom and there I would take my cue and study scripture.

Also since I had arrived late in the semester I missed any
opportunity for signing up for school sports. But my enjoyment of
scruff sandlot football would not be denied. I went up to the Clinton
Sports Shop and spoke with its Holy Cross star proprietor, Stan
Nozek, about sponsoring a junior football team made up of the
outcasts – and of those, I knew many. His generous offering was a
Spaulding game football but the rest was wonderfully thrown
together. I sought out my old Pearl Street gang adversaries. Cig
Joyce, Boozho Thompson, and Zeke Seymour, Jack Turcotte who
had gone away to Boys' Trade, Dom Ricci from my Parkhurst School
days, Al Cooperman and other assorted buddies. On Saturday
mornings, we would retire to the high school practice fields and
with odds and ends of equipment, would put each other through
intensive drills and scrimmages.

Where, then, to find a team to challenge? In those days the
only nearby town having its own high school was Lancaster. With
a limited enrollment, they fielded a six-man football team. One
afternoon I visited the high school and challenged their coach.
"Sure," he responded. "We'll give it a try." So, with a couple of
more irregular scrimmages under our belts, we donned our bits
and pieces of equipment (my own specialty was black oxford shoes
with coke bottle tops affixed to their bottoms by MagicGlue) and
appeared at the Lancaster playing field at three on a Wednesday
afternoon. We never had a chance. We didn't even know the rules.

We probably registered two first downs in the course of the afternoon and as the evening shadows lengthened the game was mercifully called off when we only trailed a mere 32—0.

But that started a minor legend in the high school that Gordon Graham pretended to be as fleet a football halfback as any who then were on the varsity. As a joke my buddies began calling me "Flash Gordon" and the challenge was laid down to the fleet varsity backs, most particularly to Bill "Nummy" Polack that "Flash Gordon" could blow him away. That was a bit much for Nummy and a contest was arranged during the midmorning break for a footrace over the 400 plus yards of the perimeter of Central Park. The whole school turned out in festive mood. The whistle blew and we were off. Nummy was just ahead of me at the first turn. But then it rapidly became no contest. At the halfway mark he led me by 50 yards and had lengthened it to 100 by the last turn. I almost fainted from exertion, falling into the arms of my chagrined supporters. But Nummy knew he was the best. He remained, for his last two years, the fastest kid in town and on my return in the 1970s, when we served together on the school committee, we exchanged great friendly jibes about that blow-out race of 1948 in Central Park. At the time, I began to realize that this humiliation brought me in from the social and athletic cold. From then on, I was an insider at Clinton High and knew I belonged.

after school

As did most other emerging teens, I eagerly sought employment after school since we were free from classes at 1:00 P.M. The fall was the season for picking apples. A quick lunch and off we would go, either by bicycle or hitching a ride out to Chandler's Orchards in Sterling or Wheeler's in Berlin. I can still smell the piquant odor of McIntosh and Red Delicious apples, fresh from the reddening early frosts.

We would pick up our ladders at the barn and off through the rows looking for the first unpicked tree. Twenty-five cents and a bushel basket was enough incentive. Point the top in an upward tree crotch, hanging by a strap with a bucket we would swing out and begin at the top working down. With any luck, by nightfall, we would have picked forty bushels. Ten dollars was a good afternoon's wages. Later in the season, we would go for the drops from which cider was made. If no one was around, you could greatly augment your crop of drops by shaking trees, pulling loose those apples negligently left behind by the pickers. And so it would go, from mid-September right up to the first week in November. A good way to put a little money away for gas if someone could only get use of his father's wheels.

At age 16, we went to Mr. O'Toole in the basement of the high school for the work permits that would get us good money in the factories. The Blackstone Plush, at the time, was heavily into an Army Duck contract procured by Congressman Philbin. Kids were not allowed near the loom machinery, but kids would work changing spools when the looms were down or pulling threads from the huge uncut carpets of duck. At $1.40 an hour, it was an easy $6.40 for an afternoon. But there were the sharpies, who wanted the pay but not the work. New to time clocks, we quickly learned how to punch each other's clocks, in and out. The varsity footballers considered that money properly theirs even when they had practice during those same work hours. So, it fell to the rest of us not only to punch ourselves in, but also punch in another card on the sly and when the foreman came around cover for our slack buddies by saying that they had just left for the Men's Room. We managed to pull it off well for most of our freshman year.

My mother constantly kept her eye open for Saturday work for "Junior." In shops or dentists offices, she would boldly assert, "I bet you have plenty of work my big son could do." Thus, I found myself at the fruit and vegetable counter of the First National right after Christmas, Saturday 8:00 to 6:00. Since it was mostly self-service, the job consisted of lugging crates and bags of potatoes from the basement cooler and spreading the produce over the shelves in the morning, then collecting it and carrying it back when the store closed. I undertook it with zeal and had a happy smile for the customers as I lorded it over the vegetables. My problem arose at the end of the day. Eager to please, I grabbed a broom and cleaned up my area, then seeing that the basement also needed a sweeping, I headed down there, briskly sweeping away. What I had failed to understand was that the manager closed his workday by playing a little footsie with the cashier. So there I was, leaning on my broom. "Anything more I can do, Mr. Derby?" I asked. Why, then, was I surprised when next Friday, Mr. Derby called my mother and they wouldn't be needing me anymore?

entrepreneurship

"Not a Soap – Not a Detergent – Magic Rinse!"

I had seen this ad running for three weeks in the Daily Item and it did the job on me for which it was intended. I was curious. What was this Magic Rinse and when was it coming? I still had the Daily Item in my hand while sitting on a bench in Central Park when "Doc" O'Malley noticed me as he walked by. I had met "Doc" the previous winter and we hit it off well. We were both stranded late at night in Boylston Center, half way home from our separate nights out in Worcester. I had gone into the cemetery to take a leak and when I came back out on Route 70, there he was. Doc got his name quite naturally. His father was a veterinarian and owned the animal hospital just off the Acre where the B & M railway trestle encountered the Berlin Tunnel. On any good Spring day, you could hear the dozens of dogs barking in the outside kennels and it was a place of excitement for growing boys. So, it was great to see Doc. He had already been out in the world. His family had no patience with public schools, so Doc was in prep school at Groton, a rather odd place for a Clinton, Irish Catholic to be educated. Perhaps that was what allowed Doc and me to connect from the very beginning.

When he was passing by me in the park, he laughed and said, "Did you see my ad?" "You mean that Magic Rinse stuff?" I asked. "Sure!" he said, "I'll bet it got your curiosity going, didn't it." "Damned right!" I responded. Doc soon explained how an Ohio classmate at Groton arranged for Doc to get the exclusive rights in Massachusetts to this new product that was basically a water softener to soften clothes before they went into the new electric dryers, making them as soft as clothes dried outside on the line. "Come on up to my garage and I'll show you," he suggested, so up we went and in his open garage bay he had set up an old-fashioned paddle washing machine. Next to the machine were barrels of paste that Doc proceeded to dump into the water in the machine. The water sloshed it around for twenty minutes and then pumped out the liquid into bottles neatly labeled, "Magic Rinse – One Quart." "I'll take you on as a partner," he offered. "I'm heading back to Ohio State in the fall and it should be taking off by then."

So began a most unlikely, but fun, partnership between Doc and me. Each afternoon (Doc never worked in the mornings) we would load four or five cases of Magic Rinse into the back of Doc's station wagon and made our rounds of the little Mom and Pop stores of central Massachusetts. Doc would enter the store and show off his teaser ad in the Item and then we would urge people to take a case on consignment – no obligation. If it sold, the store got 40%, if not we would collect it at the end of the month.

Unfortunately, Doc's heart was never in it. He was thinking only about going off to college and actually inveigled his family to send him to Paris for a month as preparation. So off he went. We had left my phone number in each store, but I received no calls. I also didn't have a way of getting around to follow up. For all I know, there may even still be a little store out there in Gardiner with a dusty old crate of Magic Rinse still waiting for a response to Doc's tantalizing ad.

CHAPTER 6
THE CONFIDENCE
TO GO FORTH

unafraid

"I, a stranger, unafraid (sic)
In a world I never made" A.E. Houseman

When I was scarcely seven years out of Clinton High, I was asked to promote non-Marxist liberalism as a guest lecturer at Davidson College, North Carolina. I had by then read James T. Farrell's Studs Lonigan trilogy and sensed parallels to Lonigan and his gang growing up in Chicago and me growing up on East Street. Farrell's gang and my gang were molded and shaped by the social and economic forces beyond their control. Indeed to this day I can never sort out how much of me is a gift from the world of my childhood. So I tailored my Davidson talk on the importance of individual courage in the face of daunting challenges facing American youth in my generation. I picked up on the title of one book of Farrell's trilogy, which he had taken from the A.E. Houseman poem "A World I never Made." As a rousing conclusion I challenged the assembled students: "As Houseman put it in his entire poem," I suggested, "we are called upon to act courageously and unafraid in that world not of our making.

The students gave me standing applause and they, the faculty and I repaired to the lounge for coffee before the first class of the day. As I basked in their obvious appreciation, the head of the English Department sidled up to me: "Good talk, Mr. Graham," he said, "but really you should check your quotes. What Houseman actually said was: "I, a stranger, *and afraid*, in a world I never made". What then was it as I grew up in a world soon to be characterized as the Age of Anxiety that allowed me to grow up secure and unafraid?

as good as anyone

That race around the park with Nummy did it. Sure I lost disastrously but I was now accepted. The jocks knew how badly I wanted to be one of them and a remarkable intervention by assistant principal Lewis "Doc" Gordon gave me the confidence to take on the most difficult of academic offerings.

"Doc" was to many an embarrassment. Only on the occasion of his tragic death some twenty years later did it come out that he was in fact gay. During our years we knew him as the English teacher who cried when he read Mark Anthony's eulogy to Caesar. We knew him as the perfect balance to the outstanding principal Eben Cobb. Cobb was a cynical Harvard man and former state rep. Doc, the effete Yale man, was given the role of bringing boys into sensitive manhood. Every boy was encouraged to join the one school fraternity – Tau Sigma – and Doc was our initiator. In preparation for our junior year Tau Sigma dinner dance, Doc started going over the basic rules of social graces. Nothing was mandated. We were simply invited to "do the acceptable thing."

If you or your date smoke, we were instructed, you must light her cigarette, but not while the car is in motion. You should pull the car to the side of the road to light up. We were told about Doc's own test of social grace. When he was invited in to pledge for his Yale fraternity, he was seated in one of two chairs in the middle of a large room. His host offered him a cigarette and a light. Then, both smoking, they chatted on a bit. Doc told us about his anxiety, as his ash grew longer. There were no ashtrays in sight. What was the host doing? Finally, he noticed the trick. That was what the cuffs on men's trousers were all about. His host was discretely dumping his ash into his cuff. Doc picked up this trick and passed it on to us – without the slightest suggestion that smoking was a good idea.

The revelation that sent a titter through the assembled boys was that should any of us find ourselves pulled over to the side of the road and wanting more than a cigarette, you must be sure you take precautions. There are devises known as condoms that you should have with you. This is to prevent the tragedy of getting this young woman pregnant. To most of course now coming up sixteen, this was not shocking news. But that there was a teacher and a counselor in our school who could speak plainly and directly to the point gave gravity to a practice which we spoke about usually only in ribald jest.

Doc's personal influence on me was both good and bad. In my sophomore year he appeared at the door of Room 13 in the Annex and asked to see me in the corridor. As we stepped outside he had a sheaf of papers in his hand. "Graham", he said, "I have here the results of the IQ tests which all of you took last fall. Your result is amazing. You have the highest IQ we have recorded here in the last ten years. We just don't understand why you are not doing better in your grades." Bad counseling! I immediately sought out our class scholar, Syd Schanberg, who indeed had sorted me out as a prime competitor since the seventh grade. "Schanberg," I bragged. "I know now that I am a lot smarter than you and I could get high nineties anytime I want. But I am not a grade-grubber. I'm going to have a good time during my high school years. I don't know about you."

In fact, I did take the challenge a bit more seriously than I let on. From then on I signed up for most of the difficult courses: Ms. Bachose's Latin III and IV, Jim Garrity's Biology , and Doc's own English course. In each of the six periods I took a course, accumulating by the end of my junior year 158 credits, just two credits short of those necessary for graduation. But I stayed on for that fourth year and it was in that year that I fully discovered the pervasive sense of upward bound democracy, the ethos of Clinton

High, going into the 1950s – that all of us in Clinton – most especially us boys of immigrant stock were "as good as anyone".

The second prophet of that doctrine was Bob "Ram" Murphy whom I first encountered in my sophomore year's course in Modern History. Bob made history come alive and related it to our little mill town through the still recent legends of Senator Walsh and Congressman Philbin. He got us into reading Time and Newsweek – with a strong provincial bias for the latter, which I explain elsewhere.

Bob's influence went far beyond his classroom. With little apparent promise of money or fame, he chose to organize a debating club at Clinton High. Looking back now, from the vantage point of the year 2000, one of the assigned debate topics seems just obsolete while the other is incredibly timely. In the school year 1949-50, we debated: "Should the American People Reject the Welfare State?" — now ancient history — but in 1950-51 we debated: "The President Should be Elected by a Direct Vote of the People." What goes around comes around!

Yet it was not the subject matter we diligently ingested in those years. It was the ethos of Bob taking us – two teams of two members each – out each weekend in his 1940 Chevy to the prime prep schools of New England, the likes of Holderness Academy in nearby New Hampshire and Milton Academy where JFK prepped for Harvard. On our trips up and back, Bob would drill us. "Look folks," he would say. "You are going to be up against poised and arrogant young men. They will be wearing blazers and rep ties. But remember you are from Clinton Mass and you are as good as anyone."

Bob's individual intervention in my life came my last year of high school. I was on a roll academically, having gradually brought my grade average close to the 85 percentile necessary to squeak into the National Honor Society. I think it was Doc Gordon, who suggested I take the national College Entrance Exam and we were all transported to Worcester's Classical High School for one of our first multiple-choice fill in blanks tests. Over the four hours I had a comfortable sense that I was finishing early and it all was a breeze. Indeed another twenty years had passed before Bob Murphy during a Memorial Day celebration in Central Park confided to me that I had got some sort of 700 plus on the verbal portion.

Knowing little or nothing about colleges, I initially applied to Boston University whose football star Harry Agannis was known to all of us. My parents were on the donator list of a fundamentalist college in Illinois, Wheaton College, whose track coach was the Olympic miler Gil Dodds. Probably because of my earlier humiliation in the footrace with Nummy I was now promoting myself as a distance runner.

My first guidance came again from Doc Gordon. He took me into the school library one day and informed me that I had made a misstep in applying to Wheaton. As a Yale man and high church Anglican the only Wheaton he knew was of course the all women's college in Norton, Mass. and Doc wanted to save me the embarrassment. He was a bit chagrined when I told him about the other Wheaton and why I wanted to go there.

But it was Bob Murphy who had the sure touch. In the top floor study hall he came up to me one noonday and said: "Gordon, I've looked over your college board scores and have you ever thought of applying to Harvard?" "What's Harvard?" was my incredible response. Bob gently explained and said he would arrange with Principal Cobb for me to take a day off and visit Cambridge. My prime concern at the time was making sure that day in Cambridge would not be counted as a day of absence. My attendance had otherwise been perfect since that ominous day in the seventh grade when my mother discovered me to be a habitual truant.

When the week came for me to take the train to Cambridge, Principal Cobb intervened in a way where I appreciated how cynicism can reach over into very helpful realism. He invited my mother up to the high school and told her frankly. "Mrs. Graham, you have a very bright son in Gordon. He is applying to Harvard, which I attended years ago. Mrs. Graham, it will be painful for you to have a son attend Harvard. He will lose whatever faith you and your husband have raised him in. He will begin looking at things quite differently. But I beg of you, Mrs. Graham, don't stand in his way." To both Eben Cobb's and my mother's everlasting credit, they had a meeting of the minds that day and the way was almost cleared for me to attend Harvard.

But then came my father's almost fatal heart attack. Within days of my acceptance to BU, Wheaton and Harvard, tragedy hit. After one of our usual high-calorie dinners, we were all gathered around the Philco listening to Lowell Thomas and the six o'clock news. Suddenly my father said: "I don't feel very good." As we turned toward him his face became white and he dropped out of his armchair to the floor. My mother ran to call the ambulance and Dr. Burke while I stood over him helpless as he gasped for breath.

The ambulance came and he was rushed to the hospital where they took him through the worst of it. But the word soon came back. Your father will never be able to go back to work – either in his menial job at Ray-O-Vac Flashlights – or indeed his passion, which was peddling his mops and patent medicines door to door. The effect of my then getting sole access to his 1948 V-8 Ford I will deal with elsewhere, but the doubts which this now cast on my attending college deserves being narrated here in its wonderful specificity.

Again it was Bob Murphy to the rescue. He soon drew out of me the details of the financial package Harvard had sent with my acceptance. I was awarded a half tuition (incredibly in the fall of 1950 Harvard's tuition was only $600) with a promise of term time 20 hours weekly employment, a $300 loan and an expectation that I would earn $500 over the intervening summer. The rest of the estimated $1800 full cost of Harvard was to come from my parents. But Bob was not satisfied that we should settle for that. The solution, he suggested, was with our Congressman Phil Philbin. "He is in his High Street Office every Saturday morning and I will make the appointment for us to see him next Saturday,"

Bob explained. I was overcome by his involvement and his willingness to go to bat for me.

When Saturday came, Bob came down in his Chevy at 9:30 and drove me up High Street to the Congressman's office over the Sugar Bowl. As we drove over Brook Street, Bob looked over and said plainly: "Gordon, you are some kind of Methodist and the Congressman, like me, is a Catholic. You are a Republican and he is a Democrat." But don't let that bother you. He wants to help anyone and if anyone can get you a better deal at Harvard, he can."

We entered an already crowded Congressional Office well before our ten o'clock appointment. About six people were there, at least two of them young men in uniform, with mothers seeking compassionate assignments for their sons at Boston Naval Base or Fort Devens. We were greeted by Mrs. Keating, the Congressman's home office secretary, whom I knew as a neighbor from the middle tenement on East Street extension. Bob Murphy and I were ushered into the office just after ten. A beaming Phil Philbin stood from behind his desk and offered his hand. We were motioned to seats and he asked what he could do for us. Bob shared the details of my story. Philbin then turned to me: "What is the tuition down there nowadays anyway, Gordon?" "Six-hundred dollars, Congressman," I responded. "Why that's outrageous! It was only $100 when I went there. The other football players and I started a laundry service. I think it's still there, it's called GoldCoast . Not only did we earn all our expenses but we each cleared $1, 000 a year."

"Mrs. Keating," he called out. "Get me Dean von Stade (the then dean of admissions) on the phone". Within minutes the connection was made and Philbin was bellowing on the phone: "Skiddy, this is T-Bone, I have this very bright young man from up here in Clinton whom you have accepted for next fall. It looks now like he can't come for financial reasons. You see his father has had a heart attack and the family is now in a bad way. When does the committee next meet? Monday, you say. OK, I'll tell him to expect to hear more from you Monday" – end of conversation.

Then Philbin turned to me and said, "Look, Gordon," I'm going back to Washington Monday afternoon but I intend to follow up on this. If you hear nothing from them by Tuesday I want you to contact me Western Union, reverse the charges."

As I left that office, I knew that I had benefited richly from the first political favor of my still young life. Of course the call came from Cambridge Monday afternoon. The scholarship was doubled to be full tuition and together with Top Boy, Syd Schanberg, I was off to Harvard and a reshaping of my life.

But it was mostly in the area of boys' athletics that Clinton's sense of parity with the world around us was emphatically imprinted on our psyches. Having my semipro football career completed by age 15, I took the next big step in spring of my junior year by going out for varsity football. Since 1945, and the return of All American, Bill McMahon (my first year Latin teacher) as coach, Clinton High went from strength to strength. "Bingo" brought a fast breaking style of T formation offense that took advantage of the small size but great speed of the children of underfed depression era immigrant parents. Sure, some of the down linemen might exceed 160 pounds but his system depended on 135-140 pound halfbacks to punch holes in the defenses of much larger players from much larger schools.

By my junior year there was already in place an experienced team composed indeed of at least some boys who had been encouraged to stay on a fifth year in high school so that we could make up in experience what we lacked in size. And experience was Bingo's program. In early spring when the frost was just out of Marhevka's Field, the call came for spring practice. The starting backfield had indeed been working as a passing unit in gym clothes on the Armory basketball court, unofficially to stay within schoolboy rules – but they had worked so intensely that they had perfected their timing long before we ran through the springtime drills. So when I put my name in, that spring of 1950, I knew it would be a long shot of even making the squad. And indeed, it was a close thing.

I was in my junior math class when the call came from Athletic Director Joe McCaffrey for boys to go to the basement supply room and pick up their uniforms. The list was alphabetical and when Joe Garofoli's name was called I waited expectantly. But the next name was Marcel Kennedy and on the list went with no Graham. All the boys filed out and were gone for about twenty minutes. As they straggled back with their duffle bags of pads, Joe McCaffrey again came to the door. "Gordon Graham," he called. "Come with me." With a warm arm around my shoulder, he led me down to the basement where Coach McMahon was standing. "We do have another uniform, Graham," he said. "Here, try on number 39." I had made the team.

The practices that spring, toward summer's end and again the week school opened were excruciating. As we wearily trod along the South Branch to the fording bridge which took us to the new field house and showers of Fuller's Field the talk was about our chances in the Midland League that year when schools like Milford and Natick had long outgrown Clinton High in size. The non-league schools like Leominster and Fitchburg were thought to have continued to play Clinton as "breathers" in their otherwise big school schedule. Then came the upcoming surprise of this Clinton's Centennial Year. For the fifth game of the schedule and in personal tribute to Coach McMahon, we were scheduled to play the prep school of his famed New York City College, Fordham. A non-league game would be done in the festival context of the town's 100th anniversary with fireworks and extra music before the whole town that Friday night.

As the season started my chance for game time now seemed slim. The backfield was already two deep in running backs and the first games were against the bigger more powerful schools. Indeed the first game against Worcester's St. Peter's School was a squeaker, where the back whose understudy I was – Joe Garofoli – scored the only touchdown. Against Milford and Natick, the Gaels were coming together, but I still remained at the end of the bench. We comfortably shut out Webster and then our minds were focused on the unknown behemoths from Manhattan New York. As they piled off their bus that Friday afternoon for their workout, we were intimidated. Their linemen clearly outweighed ours by fifteen or twenty pounds a man. We would again have to make it on luck, pluck and speed.

Our first string was ready. As we warmed up, we whooped it up, trying to psyche ourselves into confidence. But it was the field house pre game talk by Bingo that did it. "Believe me, you guys," he said. "I've been there. I've played football with the best New York City can offer. You are as good as any of them!" With that, we rushed out of the field house roaring.

From the beginning we caught Fordham on the wrong foot. Our backs just ran around their stolid line. Tom McEvilly and Jim Petricca lofted passes to Jim McNally and Red Leone just riddling the Fordham defense. We went into the Field House at half time with a comfortable lead but the first string stayed in the game and just poured it on before the 7,000 fans. As the third period moved into the final period, Bingo began substituting. Dave Hazel went in to relieve the methodical Tom McEvilly. I got anxious. This was the fifth game out of the season's ten and I needed five games to get my letter. The clock ran short into the last five minutes and we were ahead 32 to nothing. Bingo looked down the bench at me in my sparkling clean uniform. "Graham?" he hesitated. "Go in for Garofoli." As I entered the huddle I noticed the humor in Dave Hazel's eyes. "Ok," he said, "it's Graham, left half tackle trap." I just flustered. I knew he would be passing the ball off to me but I had no idea of what I was then to do with it.

The ball was snapped. I ran toward David, and he pivoted for the handoff. I just crashed into him and we both fell for a five-yard loss. He would get me for that. "OK," he said in the huddle, "It's Graham again on three. Left half off right tackle and for godsakes, Gordon, take the ball and run with it." This time I got it right. The right tackle had been neatly pushed aside by Bob Bogan after he had centered the ball. Off tackle I went leaving Bogie on the ground laughing as he saw me scamper toward the end zone. There was just one tall safety between the goal and me. As he zeroed in on me, I just pushed him deftly aside and scampered the whole twenty-six yards for the touchdown. Off went the rockets and the ariel bombs as my teammates hugged me. I forget the rest of the game, knowing only that I stood six inches off the floor in the showers. After dropping my equipment at East Street, I followed the band and the crowd in triumph up High Street, dipping down for just a few minutes into Maury's Billiards to accept the most wanted praise – that of Maury and my cousin Big Mike Vetros who really set the tone of the Real Men of the Town of Clinton. Of course if I live to be 100 I will never' be more fulfilled in life. Like John Updike's "Rabbit Angstrom," the ultimate high in life is to be found in high school sports. Bingo McMahon, like Bob Murphy, and most especially my mother Lillian Cumming Graham before them had now convinced me of Clinton's heritage – each and every one of us was as good as any of them – and then some!

I have herein – like the Jewish Sage Sirach – praised famous men and have offered as possibly representative of female teachers of my early years a couple of harridans from Parkhurst School. But there were to be found exquisitely trained and performing women scholars and mentors throughout the Clinton schools. However, it was a time of pervasive sexism and disregard for these remarkable women – symbolized and imprinted in the image of those wonderful Presentation Nuns whom I first noticed when I went uptown to school. Women (were they really women under those shapeless garments?) we saw daily as they passed on review before us four times a day as they traversed Central Park on their journey to and from St. John's Elementary School. I heard harrowing tales of how there were harpies among them as well, but on my later return to Clinton I discovered indeed as a public school committeeman that there was remarkable talent and dedication, which had never previously been discoverable across the sectarian divide of my youth.

But the nuns of the cloister impressed their image as well on the narrow minds of the school committees and administrators of

Massachusetts right up into the 1950s. Only single women need apply – and upon marriage your resignation was considered automatic.

Years later I was offered a frozen daiquiri in the modest home of one of the most dedicated of those high school teachers who gave me encouragement and direction in my formative years. "You must have thought us sexless, Gordon" she confided. "But we had our ways around it all. But I did find it a bit much to have to save up almost six months wages to go to Italy every two years or so and have a gorgeous affair with any young man who came along the strata of Naples."

But those of us who were feeling the "stirrings" readily fantasized on the inner lives of these clearly poised and worldly women. Educated in the best of women's colleges, deeply immersed in classical studies, they dominated the classrooms where they drilled into us not only the grammar of French, Latin and German which were their specialties, but also clearly lived within the worlds of Virgil, Goethe, and Hugo whose works they yearned to help us understand. Perhaps I was blessed to meet again those women when they could relate to me as a fellow adult classicist. Was it twenty years thereafter that I sat across the table from Ellen McIntyre whose 15-year-old libido she had innocently aroused those many years back. Now here we were as fellow Harvard alum, we sat across the groaning table in Worcester's Armour Museum and, being denied modern table utensils, we – using only our hands – dug into hunks of roast beef and potatoes – in a credible re enactment of a Roman orgy meal. Ellen McIntyre was a picture of grace and dignity as she readily entered into a world she could cheerfully make her own. I can only imagine what a wonderful role model the Misses Bachose, Praderio, Kerrigan and McIntyre were for the girls of the class of 1951. But I had been exposed to worldly sophistication in those formative years – and my debt to them still remains only partly repaid.

·

crest

What does any healthy American 16-year-old do with his senior year in high school? Have fun is the honest answer and in 1950-51 it was no different for me.

After that Fordham Prep touchdown and the award banquet I had crested in my athletic career. Indeed I was a bit embarrassed when Mr. Morgan the Worcester Harvard Club's alum interviewer restricted my interview to just a few questions, prime of which would I be available to the varsity in Cambridge. Harvard football had come a way down from its glory days of T-Bone Philbin and the 1924 Rose Bowl. But yes, I would make whatever contribution I could. How was I to know that the stringer for the Boston Globe had just looked at the final score of the Fordham game and put my name in on that week's Globe "All Staters."

But I was now targeted generally by those generally considered my "betters", Syd Schanberg, actually approached me to be his debate partner and to our mutual surprise we copped the state championship at Suffolk University. To his eventual distress, Syd even suggested that we room together at Harvard. His dating problems with "shiskas" by then was running parallel to mine with Jewish girls. He was deeply attracted to Sandra Sivert, a lovely daughter of a local Protestant industrialist. When he ventured to take her out in his family car, his father Louis chased him down with his store's pickup and ordered her out. Syd came, as an exile, to my home as I had, in turn, gone to stay with the Coopermans.

But it was the Cedar Hill girls with whom I was finally making time. Once my ineptitude with Trixie got known my stock with the decent girls rose. Remarkably, one of the prize queens of the Ball invited me to the Senior Girl Scout formal thus forever covering the chagrin I felt the year before when my air force reserve duty precluded me from the Junior Prom – as nasty rumors circulated that Gordon couldn't get a date.

When plans were made for a long May class weekend in New York City, I knew that I would be playing on a field familiar to me from Al Cooperman's family ties. Off we went to see Radio City Music Hall's Rockettes and a superb production starring Carol Channing of "Gentlemen Prefer Blondes" and Katherine Hepburn in "Kiss Me Kate." Since Alan didn't accompany us. I was the only guy in the crowd who could sing the lyrics of all the songs in both shows.

But the Big City led me into a rather trivial temptation, which was known to my mother and of which I am periodically reminded to this day. On one of the few hours Class Advisor Marty Gibbons afforded us, buddies Jim Arsenault, Dick Cogswell and I sauntered into one of those Times Square emporia, which specialize in fulfilling every wish of every rube new to New York. There at the rear of the store was a wonderful replica of a New York bar with cut out spaces for tourists to stick their heads through and be photographed "raising a glass" in quite sophisticated company. Jim, Dick and I were game. It must have cost all of five dollars and we each got a print. I don't recall where I secreted it when I got back to Clinton, but it was soon to reappear in the flyleaf of my battered genuine mock leather covered King James Bible.

Pasted to the Bible it was accompanied by what my mother considered her favorite quote from King Solomon's Proverbs: "Wine is a mocker/ Strong drink is raging/ and he that taketh thereof is not wise". Maybe I was Big Time in New York City, but it was Solomon who built God's Temple where someday I still hoped I would come to dwell.

lost among the saved

I had nothing to do about being raised Free Methodist. There was the tall dominating brick building in my very back yard – put there by my father's initiative. When I was brought home from Carter Memorial Hospital in late March '34, my father went over to the church and put my name – George Gordon Graham – on one of the tags hanging from the "cradle roll". It was Pastor Ross who a few weeks later came by our house and "sprinkled" me with baptism water – just to be sure I was a Free Methodist and not one of those free will adult baptizing Baptists, who were a different tribe altogether.

But baptism got you just so far with the Free Methodists. There came an age of accountability – loosely associated with confirmation or bar mitzvah, when the youngster was required to repent and give his/her heart to Jesus. And, just in case you were tempted to let the whole thing slide by, there was that great American tradition of the summer camp meeting.

For us the annual event was the Palmer Camp Meeting, held on premises rented from the First Day Adventist Church just off then major East-West Route 20 highway just West of the small town of Palmer, Massachusetts. On and off again I was taken to an ecumenically fundamentalist camping site in the woods of Douglas, MA and occasionally to "conferences," as far away as Saratoga Springs, New York, where my mother's loving sister Ellie was poisoned by the food and died. But Palmer was the mainstay year after year and the food wasn't that bad.

Our family pattern for the ten day camping period was to arrive the first Friday night when people came from their week's work and the appointed evangelist would be introduced in a happily low key prayer and praise session where personal testimonies were welcomed from the old timers of how Christ had turned their lives around. In a style later common in AA, the evening's prize went to the worst lowlife who had led a convincing numbers of years deeply in sin – until, the big event, on the basis of his mother's or wife's prayers and the ready occasion of a local evangelistic meeting – all this was left behind and rejoice with hallelujahs, this was all behind him and he had a new life. Unique among Free Methodists – and the particular personal pride of my own father – was the subsequent experience of Second Grace of Sanctification, when the recipient was protected for the balance of his/her lifetime of never again being tempted to sin. Not likely, you might say – but from my earliest childhood I had seen exactly that phenomenon in my own father's life and having skeptically scrutinized him for almost forty years I would attest to its utter authenticity.

So going to camp meeting as George Graham's son carried with it some expectations. To be left behind by George and Lillian in the hands of staff and at the mercy of a powerful evangelist became early on for me the most formidable deciding point of my life. But honestly, once my parents left on Sunday afternoon I was soon into a pattern of fun and sport. The mix at Palmer was a rich one. From Clinton there was usually my cousin Marion, quite commonly visited by older boys with cars, some of religious purpose and most with other things in mind. There were also the four Karras girls from Clinton: Doris, Mary Lou, Barbara and Loretta, who tended to be cheerful and keep out of the evangelist's way. A sprinkling from Worcester County, including my first love, Anita Stoddard, whose tragic fate I recorded previously in these pages. But it was those girls from Seekonk who stole the show.

Free Methodism was largely accorded credit for "civilizing" Seekonk, a Massachusetts suburb of Providence Rhode Island. Seekonk, like much of coastal Southern New England became a glorious melting pot of intermarriage among the Native Americans. Portuguese seamen and freed Afro-Americans with a smidgeon of opportunistic Irish thrown in. The result was tonic to my newly stirring adolescent hormones. The mix I remember was entirely females: mothers with 10-, 12-and 16-year-olds, gaily, provocatively dressed and groomed, carrying with them what to me then, and in memory now, was a promise of exotic romance. The civilization brought them by the Free Methodist missionaries was still in place, but barely. The spirituality of it all intrigued and excited them – but surely they were not going to let it get in the way of a good time. And I was there for a good time!

As the week wore on and the three a day services picked up the easy converts: those whose anxiety and guilt needed relief by promise of support in their goodness – these quickly were put on the rolls of the saved. By Thursday and Friday evening it was clear that there were going to be some holdouts – and primary among them would be those Seekonk girls and young Graham, George's boy.

One particular summer remains vivid in memory. The evangelist was a Reverend Gabriel – as in Archangel! He was a major statesman in the overall church and he had a distinguished tally of "the saved." His 20-year-old son Dick was also on staff and was successfully playing the teenage girls, most readily Cousin Marion. By Thursday night, it became obvious that there would be holdouts – those "resisting the Spirit" and the whole encampment knew who we were. On Thursday night, Reverend Gabriel preached the packaged sermon, just like last year in Allentown PA's camp grounds. "I noticed a lovely 16-year-old girl to whom I knew the Spirit was speaking. Her mother entreated. I came down into the congregation and begged her to yield to the Spirit. She had tears in her eyes. But she finally turned to me and said: not tonight! That very evening that young woman attempted to cross Highway 44 to use a pay telephone. Without warning, out of the fog came this huge tractor-trailer. The driver saw her too late and she was swept off that night into eternity – into eternity without God. Now I know that out there tonight someone is also resisting the Spirit. So we are not going to let the opportunity pass. We will sing yet two more verses of hymn 103: Why Not Tonight . . . You must be saved: why not tonight."

The aunts and widows gathered around me. Your mother and father will be back tomorrow night, they said. Their hearts will be broken when they hear that you have refused God's gracious offer. But Mrs. Tattersall at Parkhurst School had programmed me for life. I knew phoniness wherever I saw it and was willing yet once again to trust the unconditional love of my parents – and of God.

But there was a price to be paid at that encampment for my single-minded resistance. Those wonderful and superstitious Seekonk girls were carried away by the emotions swirling around us. Two of them came up to me at the end of the service and told me that Satan had appeared to them out of the woods and how could they get Jesus to protect them. Whether it was from reading my pop psych columns in the Worcester Telegram or elsewhere, I had ready a comforting answer. "There is no Satan," I said. "Those old ladies are just filling your heads with nonsense." Of course, they exposed me, however unmaliciously, and word got out. Dick, the evangelist's son stopped me outside the dining rooms. "Did you tell those Seekonk girls that there was no devil?" he challenged. "Yeah," I said, "what are you going to do about it?" Bam came his fist across my face. I never even got in a counter punch. All I could say was, "I'll tell my cousin and she'll cut you off." I really hope she did, too, but who knows, he was a very good-looking guy.

journey to faithlessness

Only in recent years have I discovered deliverance from the strait jacket which has all too often characterized adolescent "faith." I learned from somewhere in scriptural exegesis that both the Hebrew and Greek words which are commonly translated as faith meaning "belief" can just as validly be translated into the English word "trust" and that has now made all the difference.

But growing up Fundamentalist Protestant in the Free Methodist tradition did its work on me early. The unworldliness demanded and the rejection of all matters carnal somehow from the beginning undercut the positive salvation message of an incarnate God in Jesus who came into the world and lived fully as human – albeit a long time ago. Around me, I saw Roman Catholics and Jews feeling fully comfortable in this world with all its carnality. Sure there was the need for confession and the great observance of Yom Kippur, the day of contrition, but back came the Catholics and Jews, cleansed but right back at living a full life tomorrow. Baptist, Congregationalists, and Presbyterians around me – while a bit lighter in life views – were still captive to the fundamentalist demand for rejection of the world. Puritanism was in the air in Clinton – and even among the Irish branch of Catholicism, it had its grip. From my mother I was never explicitly given hints that in Anglicanism at its best there could be found a loving and accepting God.

But this was to be many years coming to the fore. From my earliest days in Sunday school and the long hortatory sermons marking every worship service, I just resisted. The Bible lessons became irrelevant fables from the beginning. I must have been four or five and home in bed with childhood mumps when my parents unwittedly provided me with a quite sophisticated set of volumes on natural history: huge illustrated books with green covers which I could hardly hold up in bed. But there were the clear and still controversial charts of Darwinian evolution – from single cells, to fish, to birds, to mammals, apes, and then Man, the end of the ape chart. There were the reconstructed skeletons of the dinosaurs – right there with their human curators standing dwarfed beside them. None of this could be reconciled with the Genesis fable of specific creation. No six-day wonders here – creation took hundreds of thousands of years – and I was as intrigued by that great mystery as I was of any the church had to offer.

There was of course the powerful effect of my cousin Marion and the other wonderfully worldly mostly girl cousins which I described elsewhere. But when Cousins Grace and Elsie Cummings took me at age four to Clinton's Strand cinema and God did not strike us dead on the spot – I knew there was another way.

Opportunities to explore alternatives were also graciously provided by my brilliant neighbor from across the street – Malcolm McLeod, from his earliest years a solid rationalist man of science. In one of our boyhood secret places – upstairs over McLeod's cluttered garage – under the eaves – reached only through a small hole in the ceiling too small to receive an adult, we read wonderful heresies together. Later on, I was told that Pageant magazine was safe and middlebrow – but not so in the early forties. For it was there that I was introduced to a non-deitistic concept of morality. An article whose logic gripped me then and has stayed with me to this day. What worth, argued the writer, of a decent and moral act if it is done in order to please a judgmental deity and to gain some afterlife reward in paradise or to escape some fearful commitment to eternal hell-fires. A better and higher morality was available, concluded the writer – it was that of the atheist or agnostic who just did the right and decent thing without expectation of favor or fear of rejection. This made marvelous and compelling sense then and I have never wavered from its compelling message in my late life ordained ministry or practice of offering spiritual direction to others.

My way back to organized religion had to await my acquaintance with the writings of Reinhold Niebuhr in my second year of college. By that time I had been captivated by the aesthetic of the Anglican Mass as performed weekly in the Cowley monastery down the Charles from Harvard. There surely was a loving and experience-expanding promise in that liturgy. But it was Niebuhr who picked up on my political reformist enthusiasms of the 1950s. He had put evolution and all the rich product of the Enlightenment, personal and social ethic together with a credible anthropology together in his great Gifford Lecture published as "The Nature and Destiny of Man." I go ahead of myself a bit, here, but it was his profoundly encapsulated concept that "Man's capacity or justice makes democracy possible; but man's inclination to injustice makes democracy necessary."

Thus, the circle was completed for me personally. The sense of original sin so fiercely fought against in my early life found its proper place in a Christian Realism, which accepted and exalted in the Saving Act of God's Incarnation.

But now looking back over the intervening years of that "unfaith journey" I can see that Amazing Grace guided my path and I had never really lost my "faith" in the trusting sense over all those years. From the moment I was brought home from Carter Memorial by unworldly but loving parents I was nurtured by the foster family Samples, surrounded by an indulgent and promiscuous cousin or two, tutored by Jews, Catholics and family boarder quasi grandparents. I experienced, in a deep and natural way, trusting love and was stimulated, in turn, to offer back love – a love which never needed a belief base – and from which I will never demand a narrow belief framework. As I approached priestly ordination I presented myself for private confession – the Common Prayer sacrament of Reconciliation. After I catalogued most of the "sins" of my sixty years of worldly life, my Confessor turned to me and said: "Gordon, I will pray for your forgiveness, but you by way of penance must promise me that for every day for the rest of your life you must recite the Book of Common Prayer of General Thanksgiving."

"We give you hearty thanks
for all the blessings of this life ...
for the means of grace and for the hope of glory ...
Give us a due sense of your mercy
that our hearts may be thankful,
and that we may praise you,
not only with our lips but in our lives."
Amen

No better life sentence could have been imposed.

payback

Mr. and Mrs. George and Lillian Graham

"Jesus went out of the house and sat beside the sea
And He told them many things in the parable, saying
Listen, a sower went out to sow some seed
And other seed fell on good soil and brought forth grain,
some a hundred fold"

Matthew 13

Those who have followed my story so far must realize how grateful I am now in later life for the love and bounty given me in those decisive formative years when it could have wound up differently. I seldom got what I deserved. I was many times over the recipient of undeserved love and given second, third, and even dozens of additional chances.

In a small way just the telling of the story is acknowledgment of the huge debt owing those loving and sacrificing parents. The family given to me: natural, fostered, boarders, neighbors, mentors, and all those cousins.

Fifteen years back I came into a little money. The hard way – the insurance payoff from a near fatal accident – is not the recommended way to get rich. But for a year or so, we were rich, this time materially, although my wife Barbara and I know well we have been enriched for many years.

However, material help does make a difference. It did when Congressman Philbin interceded for my Harvard scholarship. All those teachers who had scrimped on low pay but had never scrimped on teaching and counseling the young and wayward Gordon. That is what gave rise to the Lillian and George Graham Memorial Trust – rightly named after those two uneducated Irish immigrants who came to Clinton, found a home, and gave me my start. It was needed also to recognize that Irish connection; to acknowledge the still living American dream through which the children of immigrants can get to college and move up materially. Our children, Christopher, Nicholas and Rachel are the initial trustees of this modest fund, which already has provided for:

1. The bringing of an Irish 16-year-old—one year from the North of Ireland and on alternative years one from the West, to spend a year at Clinton High School residing with a generous host family – often from a tradition other than the youngster's own. Already 14 16-year-olds have come to Clinton under this arrangement.

2. The award each year of a $1,000 scholarship to an academically promising child of immigrants working – as did my parents in Clinton mills – to enable such a youngster to go on to a private four-year college. Several of these rare scholarships have now been awarded, most recently to children of the new immigration, from Southeast Asia.

3. A campership award each summer to a 12-year-old from a troubled family allowing that youngster to find love and support beyond his immediate family.

4. Prospectively, land interests have been acquired by the trust— small lots on opposite banks of the South Branch of the Nashua, sacred site to the young adventurous Gordon Graham, so that someday, somehow, a memorial footbridge can be built in honor of Lillian and George Graham, adventurous life pilgrims, both.